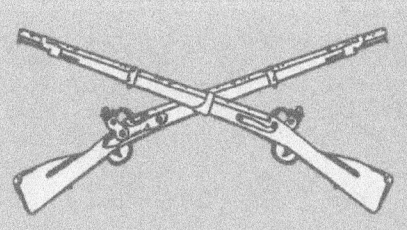

The United States Army Ground Forces During the Interwar Years 1919-1941

Infantry Cavalry Field Artillery Coast Artillery

MSG Jim Irwin (Retired)

Contents

The United States Army Ground Forces During the Interwar Years
1919-1941
Infantry Cavalry Field Artillery Coast Artillery

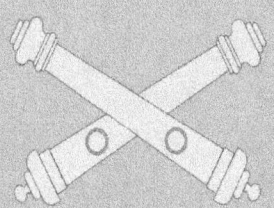 

MSG Jim Irwin (Retired)

The United States Army Ground Forces

During the Interwar Years 1919-1941

Infantry Cavalry Field Artillery Coast Artillery

BY MSG Jim Irwin (Retired)

CITI OF BOOKS

CITIOFBOOKS, INC.
3736 Eubank NE Suite A1
Albuquerque, NM 87111-3579
www.citiofbooks.com
Hotline: 1 (877) 389-2759
Fax: 1 (505) 930-7244

Ordering Information:

Quantity sales. Special discounts are available on quantity purchases by corporations, associations, and others. For details, contact the publisher at the address above.

Printed in the United States of America.

ISBN-13:	Softcover	978-1-963209-80-8
	Ebook	978-1-963209-81-5

Library of Congress Control Number: 2024904614

**This booklet is dedicated to
my father and my hero**

PFC Joseph T. Irwin

Company K, 398th Infantry Regiment

100th Infantry Division 1944-1945

THE INTERWAR ARMY
INTRODUCTION

From Bunker Hill to Baghdad, I have always been interested in United States Army history. Yet, the only area that was for so long unwritten about was the Interwar Period, the years between the World Wars. Lately there have been many new publications regarding histories of this era. I personally have gained many new insights to army units during the Interwar, including information on the great Army maneuvers of 1940 and 1941.

This booklet will cover many aspects and items pertaining to this period in American history. I have not added anecdotes as so many period histories do. This publication does provide information of units from corps, divisions, harbor defenses, and regiments. I do hope this booklet will spark an interest in you to further read and research this fascinating time in the Army of the 1920s and 30s.

This booklet can also be used as a quick reference guide for your research. The reader will find information on units, unit assignments, unit status, locations, and time periods of units have been researched by me from reliable sources. Some units may have changed stations and so the time or station will be reflected by the longest station the unit served at.

It is important to understand the Interwar Army's difficulties during the twenty years and to further understand how well it performed with the scant resources provided to it.

It is my hope that you too will gain an interest in a very important time in America's history and the struggles that the Interwar Army had to overcome.

Hat, Service M1911 (Campaign Hat) was worn by all soldiers of the Interwar Army, officer and enlisted alike, seen in many photographs of the era. In 1939 the new Garrison cap replaced the Campaign hat and was not issued to new incoming soldiers. It was easy to see that the wearing of the M1911 by Regulars as cadre for new units in essence made them "Drill Instructors." It would not be until 1964 that the Army authorized using the M1911 for wear in its Basic and Advanced training NCOs, the Drill Instructor.

"The campaign hat... was a symbol of professionalism, a mark of distinction, a personal treasure."

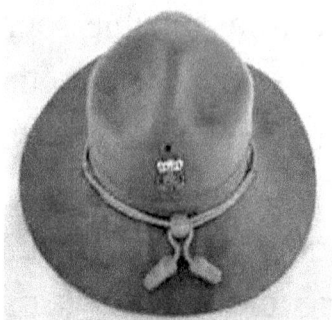

THE INTERWAR ARMY OF THE UNITED STATES

The Army of the United States prior to the Spanish American War contained some 25,000 officers and enlisted men, most performing constabulary duties in the American West.

The war with Spain put the United States on the World stage. From this time forward, America would become entangled in future hostilities worldwide. Many lessons were learned during this early experience, particularly with mobilizing and assembling troops for deployment.

With the turn of the century, America was now posting permanent garrisons to protect its overseas possessions and protectorates. The Army currently was activating new regiments to increase manpower at these overseas stations.

The United States declared war on Germany and its allies on April 6, 1917. The American Army became involved in World War I and so began the process of mobilization for action in Europe. This was to be America's first large engagement since the American Civil War. The US Army had a strength over one million men in France by May 1918. The American Expedition Force (AEF) became involved in many critical battles on the Western Front.

After hostilities ceased, most of the AEF forces returned to the United States for demobilization. However, several Regular Army divisions stayed behind in Germany for occupation duties. Many returned throughout 1919 with the last of American units leaving in 1921.

Demobilization and reassignment of Regular Army units continued up until 1922. Initially the strength of the Regular Army was set at 250,000 soldiers. This however did not come to pass, nominal strength in the Army would waiver from 120,000 to 135,000 soldiers. Most units were under-strength and dispersed throughout the Continental US and overseas garrisons, placing America with the nineteenth largest army on the world stage.

Wartime planners foresaw the next war to be waged in North America, defense strategies were built around this concept. No consideration of foreign involvement was on their agenda. America, even before the Great War, was a staunch isolationist nation. Secretary of War John W. Weeks said in 1921,

"The American people are traditionally opposed to the existence of a large standing army."

We must remember that all the United States military was segregated at this time. These units served with distinction before and throughout the Interwar period. The Army utilized native personnel from the Philippines, Puerto Rico, and Hawaii. African American soldiers had been in existence since the end of the Civil War. All these units were officered predominately by white officers.

The Army would spend the next twenty years in relatively peaceful garrison duties. Occasionally the Army was called upon to assist in labor disputes, natural disasters, protests, showcasing, and local community activities.

Two major international interventions were carried out during the interwar years by the US Army in the Far East. The first being both the 27th and 31st Infantry regiments stationed in the Philippine Islands were dispatched to Siberia during the Russian Civil War. There in Russia's eastern provinces, the two regiments were relegated for guard duty and protecting the Trans-Siberian Railroad from marauders from either Red or White units. The last units left Siberia in 1921 and returned to Manila.

Fighting broke out in Shanghai between Chinese and Japanese troops in 1932. Under orders from the President of the United States, the 31st Infantry regiment stationed in Manila was ordered to Shanghai, China to protect American lives and property within the International Settlement. The 31st along with British units in their sector maintained defensive positions and did not engage in any combat operations. The regiment stayed for five months until the threat was over, then returned to Manila.

During the Great Depression, stateside units were called upon to administer and support President Roosevelts CCC (Civilian Conservation Corp) with personnel run camps throughout the United States.

A huge demonstration in Washington, DC took place in May of 1932. Bonus Marchers, some 15,000 veterans of World War I, were demanding the early redemption of service bonuses. Camping all around the city in shanty towns and creating disturbances, the President ordered them removed. Two Regular Army regiments were ordered to clear the demonstrators. After being evicted and their camps burned down, the demonstrators left Washington, DC.

September 1, 1939, George C. Marshall was sworn in as US Army Chief of Staff. The same day Germany invaded Poland. This would be the beginning of mobilization of the US Army. The ranks grew to 13,039 officers, and 187,893 enlisted soldiers. These Regular Army soldiers would become the genesis of the now expanding Army. As new units were brought online, Regulars would serve as cadre, instructors, and mentors for newly activated units.

September 1940 found two congressional legislative acts that would increase the size of the US Army. The National Guard Mobilization Act of 1940 would place all eighteen National Guard divisions on active duty for one year. This did more than double the number of Army divisions.

The Selective Service Act of 1940 passed September 16, 1940, created Americas first peace time conscription. Men from 18 to 36 were required to register for the draft. These conscripts would increase the Army to a million men by year's end.

To test the new Army, General Headquarters (GHQ) conducted its first large scale maneuvers in September 1941. The first being in Louisiana pitting 400,000 troops of the Second and Third Armies, designed to evaluate large unit movements, logistics, leadership, and doctrine. Other maneuvers would be carried out in the Carolinas and Arkansas throughout the fall of 1941. Considered a success the GHQ maneuvers would uncover areas for improvement and provide guidance to achieve success.

Americans, many of whom were still avid isolationists felt that a new threat existed. Europe was in its second year of war and not looking good for the Allies. The intended threat of a North American invasion was on their minds. America may have felt safe for the time being, until December 7, 1941.

Civilian Conservation Corp (CCC) workers

THE INTERWAR ARMY
NATIONAL DEFENSE

The Interwar Period (1919-1941) is a page in US Army history often overlooked in history books. This period between the World Wars did not see Americans engaged in any major conflicts. Consequently, America's military was downsized considerably after the first World War. The US Army maintained a standing force during this period which was considered exceedingly small compared with other countries (19th).

The American victory over the Empire of Spain in the Spanish American War put the United States on the world stage. The American Army in the early twentieth century helped in gaining America's status as a new World Power.

CONGRESSIONAL LEGISLATION
DICK ACT 1903 (aka MILITIA ACT)

With the passage of the Dick (Militia) Act of 1903 the Federal government allotted two million dollars for improvements in the National Guard. State Guard units were permitted to obtain equipment and uniforms for their soldiers from the Federal government. National Guard officers had access to Regular Army schools. Regular Army units throughout the country aided in training for Guard units. All of this legislature was designed to integrate and train Guard units to US Army standards. Regular Army units would assist in summer encampments for Guard units.

The Act also gave the President the authority to call up the NG for nine months in the event of an invasion of the Continental US. However, the President was not authorized to send National Guard units on overseas duty (this was later dropped in 1908).

NATIONAL DEFENSE ACT OF 1916

The first National Defense Act was enacted on 3 June 1916. This legislation would update the Dick Act of 1903. It focused on the organization of the military and was particularly favorable for the National Guard. Guard unit members were now authorized a total of forty-eight paid drills per year and 15-day annual training. The law also created and the creation of an Aviation and Signal Corp in the Army. This law also provided a change in call up for Guard units. National Guard units could be federalized for up to nine months by the President. This proved useful during the Pancho Villa expedition led by the Regular Army and units of the National Guard were mobilized for duty along the Mexican border.

NATIONAL DEFENSE ACT OF 1920 (4 June 1920)

The most profound legislation during this period was the National Defense Act of 1920. The most significant was the reorganization of the Army. The Act involved enhanced roles for the National Guard and Organized Reserves. The Regular Army was still tasked with assisting training.

The National Defense Act of 1920 laid much of the groundwork for the Army of the 20s and 30s. Some of the important consequences were:

The establishment of the nine Corp Areas within the continental United States for distribution and control of interwar army units. Prior to this establishment, the Army was divided by geographical areas.

Creation of Army Air Service, Chemical and Finance Corps

Enhanced NG and Reserve role

Procurement of industries: The Army felt the frustration and confusion over equipment and supplies shortages during their mobilization process for WWI. The General Staff created committees and special departments to deal closely with America's military vendors and the US Army.

Later legislatures, particularly during the Franklin Roosevelt administration, provided New Deal programs for the Army. Works Projects Administration (WPA) and the Public Works Administration (PWA) funds were set aside for the Army, primarily for housing requirements.

US Army Continental Corp Areas

THE INTERWAR ARMY
DISTRIBUTION OF THE US ARMY

The US Army between the World Wars was known as the Inter War Army. A time of peace existed for the United States during the years from 1919 to 1941. It was also a time of steady decline and stagnation within the US military systems.

Although it had just participated in a land war in Europe and had mobilized 846,498 men for this task, once demobilizing the Army would be cut back to 228,650 by the end of 1921. Further cuts between 1922-1935 would have the Army with numbers between 133,000-146,000, ranking it nineteenth in size of the armies of the world. Of this number, 27%-29% of these forces were stationed in overseas garrisons.

America was, even before America's entry to WWI, an isolationist country. After the war, the American public and Congress wanted nothing more to do with foreign entanglements and wars. The Interwar Army was designed and distributed for defense of the continental US and its three overseas possessions.

America was still a viable force in its overseas possessions, Panama, Hawaii, and the Philippines. These garrisons were in place to protect America's interests primarily in the Far East.

The accomplishments of the Army, however, are noteworthy to say the least. With budget cuts, lack of manpower, training, and proper training facilities, Army units still functioned with professionalism and expertise.

The year 1919 found many of the Regular Army's divisions returning to the US after occupation duty in Europe. Many units were disbanded with personnel assigned to other units. Units sat at demobilization installations waiting for an assigned station; some waited up to two years.

The War Department established nine corps areas for the continental US on 20 August, 1920. These administrative headquarters assumed command for training, support, logistics, and anything not available at division levels.

There were few installations that could handle anything larger than a brigade. This required that division units would be spread out over several posts. Housing shortages made this a necessity for finding adequate space for a unit and its dependents.

Stations and garrisons throughout the interwar period were not only geographically dispersed but ranged from antique to modern installations. Many of the combat arms units found themselves in old frontier posts, old border posts, and older coastal artillery forts. Many of these older installations typically could house up to a battalion-sized unit.

Units that were deactivated were assigned to various sponsor units within a corps area or an overseas department. Some units served in a caretaker status, these units consisted of skeleton crews, detachments, companies, or sometimes individuals. Many Coast Artillery forts were placed on caretaker status during this period. Some disbanded units were assigned to colleges as ROTC instructors.

Many units were in strategic locations and housed in a manner of accommodation. Some units were stationed in or around large urban areas; the First Division's 1st Infantry Brigade had both of its regiments posted in the New York City area. Four separate regiments were posted in the Washington, DC area.

One brand new post that was established in 1918 after the war was Fort Benning, Georgia. Located in southwestern Georgia near the city of Columbus. Benning was to become the Army's Infantry Center.

With the turn of the century, the army was garrisoning units in overseas possessions and protectorates. Hawaii, Panama, and the Philippines all required housing for its soldiers and their dependents. Places like Schofield Barracks, although construction began before WWI, continued to grow during the 20s and the 30s.

The Panama Canal once open in 1914 required garrisons on both ends of the isthmus. Coast Artillery installations, a must, cropped up to protect the canal from naval seaborne attacks. Ground troops were necessary to provide mobile defense and inland installations accommodated them.

In the Philippines, the Army relied heavily on native troops to fill its military requirements. The American Army had been in the Philippines for almost 20 years prior to WWI, first fighting the Filipino insurgents.

Even though the Army had organized three active infantry divisions and one active cavalry division, the units of these units were dispersed throughout the nine corps areas of the continental United States. Only the 2nd Division had most of its units on one post for a short time at Fort Sam Houston, Texas.

The only division during this period that was stationed together on one post was the Hawaiian Division. All regiments and supporting elements were housed at Schofield Barracks in the Territory of Hawaii.

After units returned from Europe with the end of the Great War, the Army was scattered throughout the US and overseas garrisons. This was the beginning of stationing units at permanent stations. There was a strategic motive in where units were stationed. Many units were placed along the borders of Canada and Mexico.

Units were assigned to a Corps Area, and many were assigned to one of the four divisions within the continental US. The establishment of overseas divisions also assigned permanent units to their rosters. The practice of rotating units to overseas garrisons for one to four years at a time was ended prior to WWI with the stationing of permanent overseas units.

Almost all regiments at this time would spend the next twenty years at that post. Some units may have changed unit designation with just a flag exchange ceremony. A soldier could spend his whole enlistment at one post. The same was true for career soldiers, who could spend twenty to thirty years with the same unit and possibly in the same post. Officers, on the other hand, would rotate on a periodic basis for two to four years to a new station.

US Army Corps Areas and Departments 1919-1941

Corp Area/ STATION Years at
Department Headquarters Location location

1st Corps Area Boston, MA 1923-1927
Boston, MA 1933-1940
Columbia, SC 1940-1941
2nd Corps Area New York City, NY 1923-1927
Fort Jay, Governors Island, NY 1933-1940

Fort Meade, MD 1940
Wilmington, DE 1940
3rd Corps Area Baltimore, MD 1921-1922
Harrisburg, PA 1922-1927
Baltimore, MD 1933-1940
Presidio of Monterrey, CA 1940-1941
4th Corps Area Atlanta, GA 1922-1939
Fort Benning, GA 1939-1940
Camp Blanding, FL 1940
Jacksonville, FL 1940-1941
5th Corps Area Fort Thomas, KY 1922-1924
Indianapolis, IN 1924-1933
Fort Hayes, OH 1933-1940
Camp Beauregard, LA 1940-1941
6th Corps Area Chicago, IL 1922-1927
Inactive 1927-1933
Chicago, IL 1933-1940
Fort Sheridan, IL 1940-1941
Providence, RI 1941
7th Corps Area Fort Crook, NE 1920-1922
Fort Omaha, NE 1922-1929
Omaha, NE 1929-1941

Corp Area/ STATION Years at
Department Headquarters Location location

8th Corps Area Fort Sam Houston, TX 1920-1941
9th Corps Area Presidio of San Francisco, CA 1920-1941
Panama Canal Ancon, Panama Canal Zone 1917-1920
Department Quarry Heights, 1920-1941
Panama Canal Zone

Hawaiian Honolulu, Territory of Hawaii 1911-1921
Department Fort Shafter, Territory of Hawaii 1921-1941
Philippine Fort Santiago, Luzon, PI 1913-1941

Corp Area/ STATION Years at
Department Headquarters Location location

I Corp Boston, MA 1923-1927
Boston, MA 1933-1940
Columbia, SC 1940-1941
II Corp New York City, NY 1923-1927
Fort Jay, Governors Island, NY 1933-1940
Fort Meade, MD 1940
Wilmington, DE 1940
III Corp Baltimore, MD 1921-1922
Harrisburg, PA 1922-1927
Baltimore, MD 1933-1940
Presidio of Monterrey, CA 1940-1941
IV Corp Atlanta, GA 1922-1939
Fort Benning, GA 1939-1940
Camp Blanding, FL 1940
Jacksonville, FL 1940-1941
V Corp Fort Thomas, KY 1922-1924
Indianapolis, IN 1924-1933
Fort Hayes, OH 1933-1940
Camp Beauregard, LA 1940-1941
VI Corp Chicago, IL 1922-1927
Inactive 1927-1933
Chicago, IL 1933-1940
Fort Sheridan, IL 1940-1941

Providence, RI 1941
VII Corp Fort Crook, NE 1920-1922
Fort Omaha, NE 1922-1929
Omaha, NE 1929-1941
VIII Corp Fort Sam Houston, TX 1920-1941
IX Corp Presidio of San Francisco, CA 1920-1941

Interwar Forts and Posts of the US Army

Interwar Forts and Posts of the US Army	ARM	Active Status/ Closure Status	Current

Fort McClellan, Alabama TC 1915 Active Army
Fort Richardson,
Territory of Alaska CAC 1940   Active USA/USAF
Camp Pike, Arkansas INF 1917 1921 ARNG
Fort Huachuca, Arizona INF 1877 Active Army
Camp Haan, California CAC 1941 1945 USAF
Camp Kearny, California MOB 1917 1946 NAS
Fort MacArthur, California CAC 1888 1982 USAF
Fort Mason, California POE 1882 1965 NPS
Fort Ord, California MOB 1917 1994 BLM
Presidio of Monterey, California IN 1846 Active Army
Presidio of CAC 1848 1994 NPS
San Francisco, California
Fort Winfield Scott, California CAC 1912 1994 NPS
Camp Roberts, California TC 1940 1970 CANG
Fort Rosecrans, California CAC 1897 1957 NAVY
American Barracks, IN 1917 1938 *
Tientsin, China

Fort DuPont, Delaware CAC 1898 1971 SP
Fort Barrancas, Florida CAC 1739 1972 SP
Camp Blanding, Florida DC 1939 Active FLNG
Fort Benning, Georgia INF 1918 Active USA
Camp Gordon, Georgia TC 1917 Active Army
Fort McPherson Georgia IN/B 1867 1977 SP
Fort Oglethorpe, Georgia CAV 1902 1947 CD
Fort DeRussey, CAC 1904 Active Army
Territory of Hawaii
Fort Kamehameha, CAC 1915 1992 USAF
Territory of Hawaii
Interwar Forts and Posts ARM Active Status/ Current
of the US Army Closure Status

Fort Ruger, Territory of Hawaii CAC 1906 Inactive SP
Schofield Barracks, INF/D 1908 Active Army
Territory of Hawaii
Ft. Shafter, Territory of Hawaii Haw 1907 Active Army
Fort Benjamin Harrison, Indiana INF 1903 1984 SP
Fort Sheridan, Illinois IN/B 1887 1993 CD
Fort Des Moines, Iowa CAV 1900 2008 IONG
Camp Dodge, Iowa CAV 1850 Inactive IONG
Camp Funston, Kansas TC 1917 Active Army
Fort Leavenworth, Kansas CAV 1827 Active Army
Fort Riley, Kansas CAV 1851 Active Army
Fort Knox, Kentucky CAV 1918 Active Army
Camp Zachary Taylor, Kentucky TC 1917 1920 CD
Fort Thomas, Kentucky INF 1887 1994 SP
Fort Preble, Maine CAC 1808 1950 CC
Fort Williams, Maine CAC 1898 1962 CP
Fort Howard, Maryland CAC 1899 1975 CP

Fort Hoyle, Maryland FA 1922 1940 Army
Fort George C. Meade, Maryland TC 1917 Active Army
Fort Andrews, Massachusetts CAC 1901 1947 DCR
Fort Banks, Massachusetts CAC 1896 1947 CD
Fort Devens, Massachusetts TC 1917 1996 MANG
Camp Edwards, Massachusetts TC 1938 Active MANG
Fort Rodman, Massachusetts CAC 1861 1946 TP
Fort Warren, Massachusetts CAC 1833 1947 DCR
Camp Custer, Michigan TC 1917 Active MING
Fort Wayne, Michigan INF 1842 1948 TP
Fort Snelling, Minnesota IN/B 1819 Active MNNG
Camp Shelby, Mississippi TC 1917 Active MSNG
Jefferson Barracks, Missouri IN 1826 Active USAF

Interwar Forts and Posts ARM Active Status/ Current of the US Army Closure Status

Fort Leonard Wood, Missouri TC 1940 Active Army
Camp Bragg, North Carolina FA 1918 Active Army
Camp Davis, North Carolina AA 1940 1946 USMC
Fort Crook, Nebraska INF 1894 1948 USAF
Fort Constitution, New Hampshire CAC 1808 1948 SP
Fort Dix, New Jersey INF 1917 Active Army
Fort Hancock, New Jersey CAC 1806 Active Army
Camp Merritt, New Jersey POE 1917 1920 *
Fort Hamilton New York IN/D 1814 Active Army
Fort Jay, New York INF 1700s Active USCG
Madison Barracks, New York IN 1815 1947 CD
Fort Niagara, New York INF 1796 1963 SP
Fort Ontario, New York IN/B 1844 1946 SP

Camp Pine, New York/   NYNG 1908 Active Army
now Fort Drum
Plattsburgh Barracks, New York INF 1838 1957 CD
Fort Slocum, New York INF 1862 1965 TP
Fort Terry, New York CAC 1897 1954 USDA
Fort Totten, New York CAC 1862 1974 P/R
Camp Upton, New York ORTC 1917 1947 US AEC
Fort Wadsworth, New York IN/B 1847 1994 NPS
Fort H.G. Wright, New York CAC 1898 1947 CD
Fort Sill, Oklahoma FA 1869 Active Army
Fort Stevens, Oregon CAC 1863 1947 SP
Fort Amador, Panama Canal Zone CAC 1917 1999 *
Fort Clayton, Panama Canal Zone INF 1920 1999 *
Fort Davis, Panama Canal Zone INF 1920 1995 *

*Interwar Forts and Posts ARM Active Status/ Current
of the US Army Closure Status*

Fort DeLesseps, CAC 1913 1955 *
Panama Canal Zone
Camp Gaillard, Panama Canal Zone IN 1914 1927 *
Fort Gulick, Panama Canal Zone CAC 1941 1999 *
Fort Randolph, Panama Canal Zone CAC 1916 1999 *
Fort Sherman, Panama Canal Zone IN 1919 1999 *
Post of Manila, Philippine Islands D 1899 1942 *
Fort McKinley, Philippine Islands INF 1901 1949 *
Fort Mills, Philippine Islands CAC 1910 1946 *
Fort Stotenburg, Philippine Islands CAV 1919 1941 *
Fort Buchanan, Puerto Rico INF 1923 Active Army
Fort Adams, Rhode Island CAC 1798 1953 SP
Camp Jackson, South Carolina M/TS 1917 Active Army

Fort Moultrie, South Carolina CAC 1776 1947 NPS
Fort Meade, South Dakota CAV/IN 1878 1944 SP
Fort Bliss, Texas CAV 1849 Active Army
Camp Bullis, Texas IN 1917 Active Army
Fort Brown, Texas CAV 1846 1948 CC
Ft Clark, Texas CAV/B 1852 1946 CD
Fort Crocket, Texas CAC 1903 1955 CD
Fort Sam Houston, Texas IN/D 1879 Active Army
Camp Hulen, Texas TC 1925 1946 CD
Camp Robert F. L. Michie, Texas CAV 1914 1922 CD
Camp Stanley, Texas ORTC 1917 Active Army
Camp Travis, Texas TC 1917 1922 CD
Camp Wallace, Texas TC 1941 1946 CD
Fort Douglas, Utah INF 1862 1991 SC
Fort Ethan Allen, Vermont CAV 1894 1944 CD
Camp Lee, Virginia TC 1917 Active Army
Fort Monroe, Virginia CAC 1808 Active USA
Fort Myer, Virginia CAV 1863 Active Army
Camp Pendleton, Virginia NG 1912 1942 NGB
Interwar Forts and Posts ARM Active Status/ Current of the US Army Closure Status

Fort Story, Virginia CAC 1914 Active Army
Fort Lewis, Washington FA/D 1917 Active Army
Vancouver Barracks, Washington INF 1849 2011 NPS
Fort Worden, Washington CAC 1902 1953 SP
Fort George Wright, Washington INF 1899 1957 CC
Fort Francis E. Warren, Wyoming IN/B 1930 1947 USAF
Fort D.A. Russell, Wyoming CAV 1867 1927 *

* Returned to Sovereign Nation NGB National Guard Bureau

** Fort Francis E. Warren/name change NPS National Park Service
AA Anti-Aircraft M Mobilization Site
B Brigade ORTC Organized Reserve
Training Camp
BLM Bureau Land Management POE Port of Embarkation
CAC Coast Artillery Corp PR Parks and Recreation
CC Community College SC State College
CD Civilian Development SP State Park
CP Community Park TC Training Camp
D Division Headquarters TP Town park
DC Division Camp US AEC Atomic Energy
Commission
DCR Dept. of Conservation USAF US Air Force
and Recreation
FA Field Artillery USCG US Coast Guard
HD Hawaiian Department USDA US Dept of Agriculture
NAS Naval Air Station USMC US Marine Corp
NG   National Guard

US Army Manpower 1919-1941					
Year	Total Army Strength	Year	Total Army Strength	Year	Total Army Strength
1919	846,498	1927	133,268	1935	137,966
1920	201,918	1928	134,505	1936	166,123
1921	228,650	1929	137,529	1937	178,108
1922	146,507	1930	137,337	1938	183,455
1923	131,254	1931	138,817	1939	187,893
1924	140,943	1932	132,399	1940	267,767
1925	135,254	1933	135,015	1941	1,461,000
1926	133,443	1934	136,975		

THE INTERWAR ARMY DIVISIONS

The United States Army at the turn of the twentieth century contained no standing divisions. Prior to the establishment of parent divisions, Army units were controlled through Army Departments throughout the continental US. Historically divisions were created by Congress when required, such as in time of conflict or war.

Congress authorized the first division in 1916, thus becoming the base element for the US Army. The Provincial Division was organized for General Pershing and his expedition into Mexico searching for Pancho Villa. The Provincial division was made up of Regular and National Guard troops from several states.

With America's entry into the First World War, the Army began at organizing divisions to join the fight in Europe. By Armistice Day the Army had created 62 Divisions. Forty-two of these divisions deployed overseas, twenty-nine had served on the Western Front (7 Regular Army, 11 National Guard, 11 National Army).

The US Army developed what was known as the Square division. The Square division consisted of three brigades: two infantry and one field artillery brigade along with support/ service regiments. The Infantry brigades contained two infantry regiments which contained three battalions. The field artillery brigade would contain two and some cases three field artillery regiments of two battalions each. Support regiments for the division included an engineer, quartermaster, and medical regiments.

With the passage of the National Defense Act of 1920 the Army's size was limited to 228,650 personnel. This number was never maintained during the 1920s and 1930s. Actual size wavered from 133,000 to 146,000 personnel Army wide. Among these numbers, 27 to 29 percent were stationed in overseas garrisons.

Regular Army divisions consisted of divisions, the 1st to the 9th. The 1st, 2nd, and 3rd were active divisions. The 4th to the 9th were configured as RAI (Regular Army Inactive). One cavalry division (1st Cavalry Division) was activated in the US. Overseas divisions included the Panama, Hawaiian and Philippine Divisions.

First Division units were assigned to 1st, 2nd, and 4th Corp Areas.

1st Infantry Brigade concentrated its units in the New York City area.

Second Infantry Brigade units were scattered across northern New York state along the Great Lakes facing the Canadian border.

1st Field Artillery Brigade units were in Vermont and Maryland.

Support units were spread out, 1st Engineer Regiment stationed at Fort DuPont in Delaware, 1st Medical Regiment at Carlisle Barracks in Pennsylvania, and the 1st Quartermaster Regiment at Fort Hamilton New York, Second Division, after returning from Europe was stationed at Fort Sam Houston within Eight Corp Area. It was the only division in the continental United States that was posted in its entirety. In 1927, due to housing shortages the divisions 4th Infantry Brigade was posted to Fort Warren in Wyoming placing the brigade in Ninth Corp Area. Third Infantry Brigade remained at Fort Sam Houston along with the divisions field artillery and support units.

The division was used many times during the interwar period as a test division. New and innovative practices and concepts were tested by 2nd Division soldiers.

3rd Division units were stationed in the western portion of the United States within the boundaries of Ninth Corp Area. The division's 5th Infantry Brigade was in the northwest section of 9th Corp Area at Vancouver Barracks and Fort Lewis Washington. Sixth Infantry Brigade units occupied stations in the southern section of Ninth Corp Area with brigade headquarters located at Fort Douglas, Utah. Third Field Artillery Brigade was headquartered at Fort Lewis.

DIVISION ACTIVATIONS

Four US Army divisions were organized in 1921.

First Cavalry Division was formed 20 August 1921 to serve predominantly along the US-Mexico border. It consisted of two Cavalry Brigades with two cavalry regiments assigned to each. Each cavalry regiment contained two squadrons. The division was light on field artillery, containing only one squadron for the whole division. Support units included engineer, quartermaster, and medical regiments.

Constituted 3 June 1921, the Panama Canal Division consisted of 19th and 20th Infantry Brigades. The 19th consisted of two regiments: 14th Infantry located on the Atlantic side of the canal and the 33rd Infantry located at the Pacific side of the canal. The 20th Brigade located in Puerto Rico consisted of two regiments, the 42nd and 65th Infantry Regiments, both made up of Puerto Rican regulars. Field artillery assets consisted of one battalion in the Canal Zone.

The Hawaiian Division established 1 February 1921, was located at Schofield Barracks T.H. The division contained two infantry (21st and 22nd Infantry Brigades) and an ArtilleryBrigade (11th Field Artillery Brigade) plus supporting units. The only division in the interwar period to be fully manned and stationed at the same post. The division's mission was protection of America's forward base in the Pacific, mainly the protection of Pearl Harbor.

Constituted on 7 Dec. 1922, the Philippine Division was made up of US Army Regulars and Philippine natives (Philippine Scouts). The 23rd Infantry Brigade was formed using two Philippine Scout regiments, the 45th and 57th Infantry regiments. The 24th Infantry Brigade consisted of Regular Infantry Regiments, the 31st Infantry Regiment, and 1st Battalion 15th Infantry Regiment. The 24th Brigade was deactivated in 1930. Division artillery consisted of one artillery regiment. The 23rd Infantry Brigade and its supporting elements were stationed close to Manila at Fort William McKinley.

Divisions, the Fourth to the Ninth were organized as RAI divisions. The even numbered Infantry Brigades (8th, 10th, 12th, 14th, 16th, and 18th) of the afore mentioned divisions were partially organized as a Brigade representing their parent division. Infantry Brigade's represented the division in an inactivated status. Brigades consisted of two active infantry regiments and scaled down supporting artillery, engineer, and support elements.

Although some units changed location and status, all these Divisions would remain the same for the next twenty years.

REGULAR ARMY
ACTIVE DIVISIONS
1919-1941

 1st Division

 Panama Division

 2nd Division

 1st Cavalry Division

 Hawaiian Division

 3rd Division

 Philippine Division

REGULAR ARMY
INACTIVE (RAI)
DIVISIONS
1919-1941

 4th Division RAI

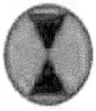 7th Division RAI

 5th Division RAI

 8th Division RAI

 6th Division RAI

 9th Division RAI

Infantry Division 1921

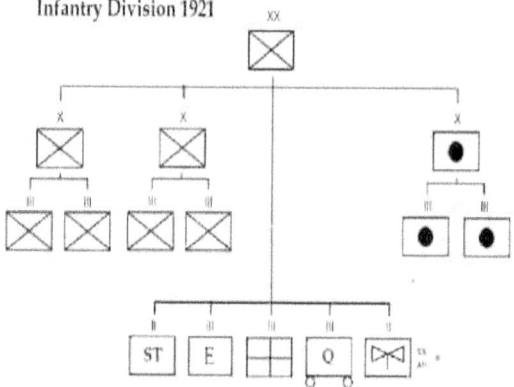

Infantry Brigade 1921

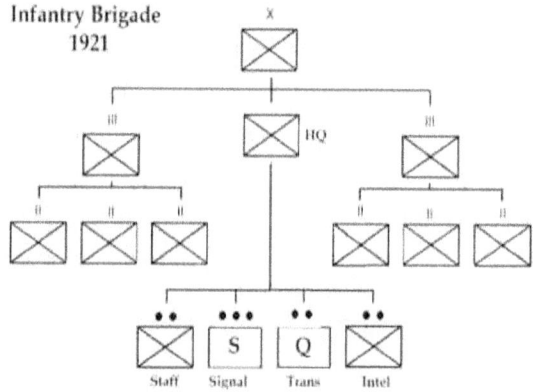

Cavalry Division 1921

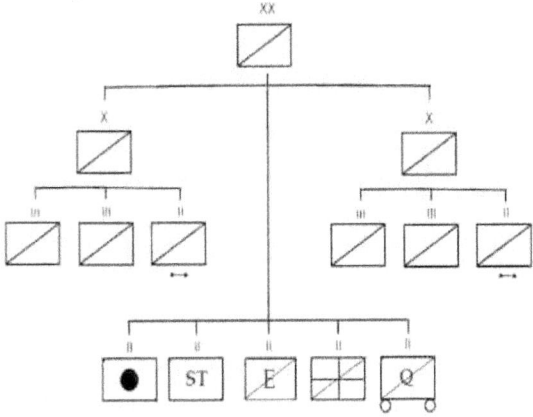

Cavalry Brigade 1921

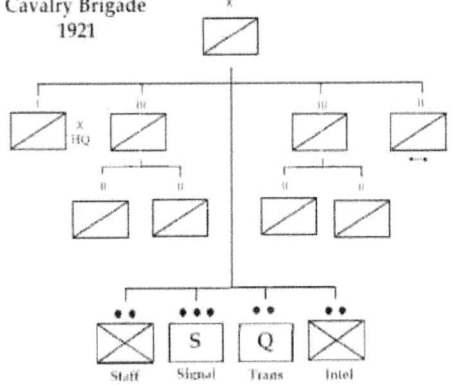

 1st Division
Fort Hamilton, NY
1922-1939

 1st Infantry Brigade
Fort Wadsworth, NY

2nd Infantry Brigade
Fort Ontario, NY

 16th Infantry
Fort Jay, NY

26th Infantry
Plattsburgh
Barracks, NY

 18th Infantry
Fort Hamilton, NY

28th Infantry
Fort Niagara, NY

 1st Field Artillery
Brigade
Fort Hoyle, MD

1st Engineer
Regiment
Fort Dupont, DE

 6th Field Artillery
Regiment
Fort Hoyle, MD

1st Quartermaster
Regiment
Fort Hamilton, NY

 7th Field Artillery
Regiment
Fort Ethan Allen, VT

1st Medical Regiment
Carlisle Barracks, PA

First Division
Unit 1919-1941 Location Date/s Status of unit
7 Dec 1941-

1st Division HQ/HHC Cp. Zachary Taylor, KY 3 Sep 1919-
Camp Dix, NJ Oct 1920-
Fort Hamilton, NY 6 Jun 1922-
Div. converts triangular Oct 1939-

Fort Benning, GA Nov 1939-
Fort Hamilton, NY Aug 1940-
Camp Devens, MA Feb 41
7 Dec. 1941

1st Infantry HQ/HHC Cp. Zachary Taylor, KY 3 Sep 1919-
Brigade Camp Dix, NJ Sep 1920-
Fort Wadsworth, NY 19 Sep 22-
New York City, NY 23 Mar 1925-
Camp Dix, NJ 10 Oct 1931-
New York City, NY 8 Apr 1933-
Fort Wadsworth, NY 29 Aug 1935-
Disbanded 21 Apr 1938- Disbanded

16th Infantry HQ/HHC Cp. Zachary Taylor, KY 4 Oct 1919-
Regiment 1st and Camp Dix, NJ 16 Sep 1920-
2nd BNs Fort Jay, NY 10 Jun 1922-
Fort Benning, GA 9 Nov 1939-
Fort Jay, NY 1 May 1940-
Camp Devens, MA 20 Feb 1941. 1st Division
3rd BN Zachary Taylor, KY 4 Oct 1919-
Camp Dix, NJ 16 Sep 1920-
Fort Jay, NY 10 Jun 1922-
Fort Wadsworth, NY 1 Sep 1922-
Fort Jay, NY 18 Mar 1933-
Fort Benning, GA 9 Nov 1939-
Fort Jay, NY 1 May 1940-
Camp Devens, MA 20 Feb 1941.
7 Dec. 1941 1st Division
18th Infantry HQ/HHC Cp. Zachary Taylor, KY 4 Oct 1919-
Regiment 1st BN Camp Dix, NJ 16 Sep 1920-
" Fort Slocum, NY 10 Sep 1922-
HHC Fort Hamilton, NY 10 Jan 1928-
Fort Benning, GA 9 Nov 1939-
Fort Slocum, NY 1 May 1940-
Camp Devens, MA 27 Feb 1941. 1st Division

18th Infantry 2n BN Cp. Zachary Taylor, KY 4 Oct 1919-
Regiment Camp Dix, NJ 16 Sep 1920-
Fort Schuyler, NY 10 Sep 1922-
Fort Slocum, NY 10 Jan 1928-
Fort Benning, GA 9 Nov 1939-
Fort Slocum, NY 1 May 1940-
Camp Devens, MA 27 Feb 1941. 1st Division
3rd BN Cp. Zachary Taylor, KY 4 Oct 1919-
Camp Dix, NJ 16 Sep 1920-
Fort Hamilton, NY 0 Sep 1922-
Fort Wadsworth, NY Apr 1933-
Fort Benning, GA Nov 1939-
Fort Wadsworth, NY 1 May 1940-
Camp Devens, MA 27 Feb 1941.
7 Dec. 1941 1st Division

2nd Infantry HQ/HHC Cp. Zachary Taylor, KY 3 Sep 1919-
Brigade Camp Dix, NJ Oct 1920-
Madison Barracks, NY Jul 1922-
Fort Ontario, NY 15 Oct 1931-
Disbanded 11 Oct 1939- Disbanded

26th Infantry HQ/HHC Cp. Zachary Taylor, KY 4 Oct 1919-
Regiment 1st and Camp Dix, NJ 10 Sep 1920-
3rd BNs Plattsburgh Barracks, NY 4 Jul 1922-
Fort Benning, GA 1 Oct 1939-
Plattsburgh Barracks, NY 5 Jun 1940-
Camp Devens, MA 27 Feb 1941. 1st Division
2nd BN Cp. Zachary Taylor, KY 4 Oct 1919-
Camp Dix, NJ 10 Sep 1920-
Plattsburgh Barracks, NY 4 Jul 1922-

Fort Benning, GA 1 Oct 1939-
Plattsburgh Barracks, NY 5 Jun 1940-
Camp Devens, MA 1 Aug 1940.
7 Dec. 1941 1st Division

28th Infantry HQ/HHC Cp. Zachary Taylor, KY 4 Oct 1919-
Regiment 2nd BN Camp Dix, NJ 12 Sep 1920-
Fort Niagara, NY 16 Oct 1939.
Relieved from 1st Div. 16 Oct 1939. Assigned to
Fort Jackson, SC 2 Dec 1940- 8th Division
7 Dec. 1941 22 Jun 1940.

28th Infantry 1st BN Cp. Zachary Taylor, KY 4 Oct 1919-
Regiment Camp Dix, NJ 26 Jun 1922-
Fort Porter, NY 1 Oct 1926-
Madison Barracks, NY 15 Oct 1931
Fort Hayes, OH 30 Sep 1933- Assigned to
Inactivated at Ft Hayes 16 Oct 1939. 8th Division
Relieved from 1st Div. 22 Jun 1940.
3rd BN Cp. Zachary Taylor, KY 4 Oct 1919-
Camp Dix, NJ 12 Sep 1920- Assigned to
Fort Ontario, NY 22 Jun 1922- 8th Division
Relieved from 1st Div. 16 Oct 1939. 22 Jun 1940.

1st Field HQ/HHB Cp. Zachary Taylor, KY 4 Oct 1919-
ArtilleryBrigade Camp Dix, NJ 26 Sep 1920-
Montauk Point, NY May 1922-
Fort Hoyle, MD 18 Oct 1922-
Disbanded 16 Oct 1939- Disbanded

6th Field Artillery HQ/HHB Cp. Zachary Taylor, KY 4 Oct 1919-
Regiment Camp Dix, NJ 24 Sep 1920-
1st Fort Hoyle, MD 25 Sep 1922- Assigned to
Relieved from 1st Div. 16 Oct 1939. 8th Division

Relieved from 8th Div. 20 Jul 1940- 22 Jun 1940.
Inactivated - 1st BN. 1 Aug. 1940-
Reorganized & redesignated 4-Jan-41 6th FAB
7 Dec 1941- 1st Division

7th Field Artillery HQ/HHB Cp. Zachary Taylor, KY 4 Oct 1919-
Regiment Camp Dix, NJ 24 Sep 1920-
1stBN Fort Ethan Allen, VT 29 May 1922. 7th FAB
2nd BN Cp. Zachary Taylor, KY 4 Oct 1919- 32nd FAB
Camp Dix, NJ 24 Sep 1920-
Madison Barracks, NY 5 Sep 1922.
Inactivated 1 Dec 1934.
Organized Fort Ethan Allen, 3rd BN VT 1 Jun 1940- 33rd FAB
Reorganized and redesignated   1 Oct 1940-
7 Dec 1941- 1st Division

1st Engineer HQ/HHC Cp. Zachary Taylor, KY 4 Oct 1919-
Regiment Camp Dix, NJ 16 Sep 1920-
Fort DuPont, DE 1 Sep 1922.
Disbanded 16 Oct 1939.
1st BN Redesignated 12 Oct 1939. 1st Eng. Bn.
2nd BN Redesignated 9 Oct 1939. 27th Eng. Bn.

1st Medical HQ/HHC Cp. Zachary Taylor, KY 4 Oct 1919- 1st Division
Regiment Camp Dix, NJ 16 Sep 1920-
Carlisle Barracks, PA 25 Jun 1922.
Disbanded 8 Oct 1939.

1st HQ/HHC Camp Dix, NJ 23 Mar 1921-
Quartermaster Fort Wadsworth, NY 30 Sep 1922-
Regiment Fort Jay, NY 13 Nov 1923-
Fort Hamilton, NY 6 Mar 1928-
Inactivated 15 Jun 1931-
Redesignated 1st Bn.,   1 May 1936-
1st QM

Relieved from 8 Oct 1939
1st Division

1st Battalion 28th Infantry Regiment 1931
Maddison Barracks, New York

2nd Division
Fort Sam Houston, Texas
1919-1941

3rd Infantry Brigade Fort Sam Houston, Texas 1922-1939	4th Infantry Brigade Fort Warren, Wyoming 1927-1939

 9th Infantry
Fort Sam Houston
Texas

 1st Infantry
Fort Warren, WY

 23rd Infantry
Fort Sam Houston
Texas

 20th Infantry
Fort Warren, WY

2nd Field Artillery Brigade
Fort Sam Houston, Texas
1923-1939

2nd Engineer Regiment
Fort Logan, Colorado

 12th Field Artillery
Regiment
Fort Sam Houston, Texas

2nd Quartermaster
Regiment
Fort Sam Houston, Texas

15th Field Artillery
Regiment
Fort Sam Houston, Texas

2nd Medical Regiment
Fort Sam Houston, Texas

Second Division

Unit	1919-1941 Location	Date/s	Status of unit 7 Dec 1941-
2nd HQ/HHC	Camp Travis, TX	16 Aug. 1919-	
Division	Fort Sam Houston, TX	13 Dec. 1922-	
Division converts triangular		Oct. 1939- 7 Dec 1941	

3rd HQ/HHC Camp Travis, TX 16 Aug. 1919-
Infantry Fort Sam Houston, TX 13 Dec. 1922-
Brigade Disbanded 9 Oct. 1939 Disbanded

9th HQ/HHC Camp Travis, TX 16 Aug 1919-
Infantry Fort Sam Houston, TX 12 Dec 1922-
Regiment 7 Dec 1941. 2nd Division

23rd HQ/HHC Fort Sam Houston, TX 16 Aug 1919-
Infantry
Regiment 7 Dec 1941. 2nd Division

4th Infantry HQ/HHC Camp Travis, TX 4 Oct. 1920
Brigade Fort Sam Houston, TX 13 Dec 1922-
Fort D.A. Russell, WY 28 Jun. 1927
Disbanded 16 Oct. 1939 Disbanded

1st Infantry HQ/HHC Camp Lewis, WA 1 Jun 1919-
Regiment Fort Sam Houston, TX 27 Jul 1921-
Fort Francis Warren, WY 28 Jun 1927-
Relieved from 2nd Division 16 Oct 1939. Assigned to
Fort Leonard Wood, MO May. 1940 6th Division
7 Dec 1941.

20th Infantry HQ/HHC Fort Riley, KA 1 Jun 1919-
Regiment Fort Crook, NB 1 Jul 1919-
Fort Sam Houston, TX 29 Sep 1920-
Fort Sill, OK 1 Mar 1925-
Fort Francis Warren, WY 28 Jun 1927-
Relieved from 2nd Division 16 Oct 1939. Assigned to
1st BN Fort Riley, KA 1 Jun 1919- 6th Division
Fort Brady, MI 1 Jul 1919-
Fort Sam Houston, TX 29 Sep 1920-
Fort Francis Warren, WY 28 Jun 1927-

Relieved from 2nd Division 16 Oct 1939. Assigned to
2nd BN Fort Riley, KA 1 Jun 1919- 6th Division
Fort Benjamin Harrison, IN 1 Jul 1919-
Fort Sam Houston, TX 29 Sep 1920-
Fort Francis Warren, WY 28 Jun 1927-
Relieved from 2nd Division 16 Oct 1939.
20th Infantry 3rd BN Fort Riley, KA 1 Jun 1919-
Regiment Fort Crook, NB 1 Jul 1919-
Fort Sam Houston, TX 29 Sep 1920-
Fort Sill, OK 1 Mar 1925-
Fort Francis Warren, WY 28 Jun 1927-
Relieved from 2nd Division 16 Oct 1939. Assigned to
Fort Jackson, SC 17 Nov. 1939 6th Division
Fort Francis Warren, WY 28 May. 1940
Fort Leonard Wood, MO 20 May. 1941
7 Dec 1941.

2nd Field HQ/HHB Camp Travis, TX 16 Aug. 1919-
Artillery Brigade Fort Sam Houston, TX Dec. 1923-
Disbanded 7 Oct. 1939 Disbanded

12th FA HQ/HHB Camp Travis, TX 16 Aug 1919-
Regiment Fort Sam Houston, TX 24 Sep 1920-
Reorganized and Redesignated 1 Oct 1940. 12th FAB
7 Dec 1941. 2nd Division
15th FA HQ/HHB Camp Travis, TX 4 Aug 1919-
Regiment Fort Sam Houston, TX 24 Sep 1920-
Inactivated less 2nd BN 31 Oct. 1929
Reactivated at Fort Sam 1 Dec 1934
1stBN Houston, TX 24 Sep 1920-
Inactive 1929-1934.
2nd BN Fort Sam Houston, TX 24 Sep 1920-
Reactivated at Fort Sam Hou- 1 Dec 1934.
Reorganized and Redesignated 1 Oct 1940. 15th FAB
7 Dec 1941. 2nd Division

2nd Engineer HQ/HHC Camp Travis, TX 16 Aug 1919-
Regiment Fort Sam Houston, TX 12 Dec 1922-
Fort Logan, CO 14 Jun 1927-
Disbanded 16 Oct 1939.
1st BN Camp Travis, TX 16 Aug 1919-
Fort Sam Houston, TX 12 Dec 1922-
Fort Logan, CO 14 Jun 1927-
Reorganized and 12 Oct 1939. 2nd Eng. Bn.
Redesignated
2nd BN Camp Travis, TX 16 Aug 1919- 2nd Division Fort Sam Houston, TX 12 Dec 1922-
Fort Logan, CO 14 Jun 1927-
Inactivated 1 Aug 1933-
Disbanded 16 Oct 1939.

2nd Medical HQ/HHC Camp Travis, TX 11 Aug 1919-
Regiment Fort Sam Houston, TX 1 Jun 1922-
Reorganized and Redesignated   10 Oct 1939.   2nd Medical Bn 7 Dec 1941. 2nd Division

2nd HQ/HHC Camp Travis, Texas 11 Aug. 1919-
Quartermaster Fort Sam Houston, TX Jun 1922-
Regiment Inactivated 30 Jun. 1931-
Disbanded 7 Oct 1939. Reorganized and Redesignated 1 May 1936- 2nd QM Bn.
7 Dec 1941. 2nd Division

Fort Sam Houston, Texas
Home of Second Division 1919-1941

3rd Division
Fort Lewis, Washington
1921-1941

5th Infantry Brigade
Vancouver Barracks, WA

6th Infantry Brigade
Fort Douglas, Utah

4th Infantry
Fort Wright, WA

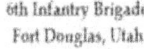 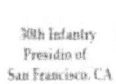 
30th Infantry
Presidio of
San Francisco, CA

7th Infantry
Vancouver
Barracks, WA

38th Infantry
Fort Douglas,
Utah

3rd Field Artillery
Brigade
Fort Lewis, WA

6th Engineer
Regiment
Fort Lawton, WA

10th Field Artillery
Regiment
Fort Lewis, WA

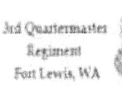
3rd Quartermaster
Regiment
Fort Lewis, WA

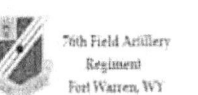
76th Field Artillery
Regiment
Fort Warren, WY

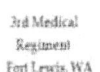
3rd Medical
Regiment
Fort Lewis, WA

Third Division

Unit 1919-1941 Location Date/s Status of unit
7 Dec 1941-
3rd HQ/HHC Camp Pike, AR 31 Aug. 1919-
Division Camp Lewis, WA 3 Sep 1921-
Division converts triangular Oct. 1939-
Camp Lewis, WA 7 Dec. 1941-

5th Infantry HQ/HHC Camp Pike, AR 15 Sep. 1919-
Brigade Camp Lewis, WA 20 Sep. 1921-
Vancouver Barracks, WA 27 Sep 1922-
Disbanded 16 Oct. 1939- Disbanded

4th Infantry HQ/ Camp Pike, AR 30 Aug 1919- Alaskan
Regiment 2nd BN Camp Lewis, WA 20 Sep 1921- Defense
Fort George Wright, WA 21 Jun 1922- Command
Fort Lewis, WA 1 Dec 1939-
Relieved from 3 Div. 14 May 1940- Anchorage
1st BN Camp Pike, AR 30 Aug 1919-
Fort Lewis, WA 20 Sep 1921-
Fort Missoula, MT 21 Jun 1922-
Camp Lewis, WA 1 Dec 1939-
Relieved from 3 Div. 14 May 1940- Anchorage
3rd BN Camp Pike, AR 30 Aug 1919-
Fort Lewis, WA 20 Sep 1921-
Fort Lawton, WA 21 Jun 1922-
Fort Lincoln, ND 11 Oct 1927-
Relieved from 3 Div. 14 May 1940- Chilkoot

7th Infantry HQ/ Camp Pike, AR 27 Aug 1919-
Regiment 1st and Camp Lewis, WA 20 Sep 1921-
3rd BNs Vancouver Barracks, WA 27 Sep 1922-
Fort Lewis, WA 7 Feb 1941-
2n BN Camp Pike, AR 27 Aug 1919-
Camp Lewis, WA 20 Sep 1921-
Chilkoot Barracks, TA 27 Sep 1922-
Camp Bonneville, ID 18 Oct 1939-
Vancouver Barracks, WA 7 May 1940-
Fort Lewis, WA 7 Feb 1941-
7 Dec. 1941- 3rd Division

6th Infantry HQ/HHC Camp Pike, AR Sep 1919-
Brigade Camp Lewis, WA 21 Sep. 1921-
Fort Douglas, UT 9 Jun. 1922-

Fort Rosecrans, CA 27 Dec. 1927-
Fort Douglas, UT 8 Oct 1931-
Disbanded 12 Oct 1939- Disbanded

30th Infantry HQ/HHC Camp Pike, AR 26 Aug 1919-
Regiment   Presidio of San Francisco, CA 30 Aug 1922-
Fort Ord, CA 5 Jan 1940-
Relieved from 3rd Div. 12 Jan 1940-
Presidio/ San Francisco, CA 15 May 1940-
Fort Lewis, WA 31 Mar 1941. 3rd Division

38th Infantry HQ/HHC Camp Pike, AR 23 Aug 1919-
Regiment 2nd and Camp Lewis, WA 16 Sep 1921-
3rd BNs Fort Douglas, UT 6 Jun 1922-
Relieved from 3rd Div. 12 Oct 1939- 2nd Division
1st BN Camp Pike, AR 23 Aug 1919-
Camp Lewis, WA 16 Sep 1921-
Fort Logan, CO 6 Jun 1922-
Fort Sill, OK 1 Jun 1927-
Inactivated 1 Oct 1933-
Activated 1 May 1939-
Relieved from 3rd Div. 12 Oct 1939-
Assigned to 2nd Division 12 Oct 1939-
Camp Bullis, TX 9 Nov 1939-
Fort Sam Houston, TX 24 Feb 1941-
7 Dec 1941- 2nd Division

3rd Field HQ/HHB Camp Pike, AR 25 Aug 1919-
Artillery Camp Lewis, WA 11 Aug 1921-
Brigade Disbanded 16 Oct 1939- Disbanded

10 Field HQ/HHB Camp Pike, AR 27 Aug 1919-
Artillery Camp Lewis, WA 15 Sep 1921-
Regiment

10 Field 3rd BN   Activated at Fort Lewis, WA 12 Oct 1939-

Artillery Reorganized and Redesignated 1 Oct 1940.   10th FAB
Regiment   7 Dec 1941-   3rd Division

76th Field HQ/HHB Camp Pike, AR 29 Aug 1919-
Artillery 1stBN Camp Lewis, WA 21 Sep 1921-
Regiment Fort Francis Warren, WY 28 Jun 1922-
Relieved from 3rd Div. 16 Oct 1939.
Reorganized and Redesignated 22 Jan 1941.   76th FAB
2nd BN Camp Pike, AR 29 Aug 1919-
Camp Lewis, WA 21 Sep 1921-
Presidio of Monterey, CA 21 Aug 1922-
Relieved from 3rd Div.   16 Oct 1939.   7th Division

6th Engineer HQ/HHC Camp Pike, AR 30 Aug 1919-
Regiment 1st BN Camp Lewis, WA 21 Sep 1921-
Fort Lawton, WA 8 Oct 1927-
Reorganized and Redesignated 12 Oct 1939.   6th Eng. Bn.
Regiment disbanded 12 Oct 1939.
2nd BN Camp Pike, AR 30 Aug 1919-
Camp Lewis, WA 21 Sep 1921-
Fort Winfield Scott, CA 1 May 1922-
Reorganized and Redesignated   13 Oct 1939.   10th Eng. Bn.
Relieved from 3rd Div. 13 Oct 1939.

3rd Medical HQ/HHC Camp Pike, AR 31 Aug 1919-
Regiment Camp Lewis, WA 21 Sep 1921-
Inactivated 31 Oct 1922-
Presidio/San Francisco, CA 13 Oct 1939.
Reorganized and Redesignated 13 Oct 1939.   3rd Med. Bn.

3rd HQ/HHC Camp Pike, AR 26 Mar 1921-
Quartermaster Camp Lewis, WA 15 Sep 1921-
Regiment Inactivated 20 May 1931-
Activate 1st Bn, 3rd QM Regiment
1 May 1936-
Disbanded 12 Oct 1939.

1st Cavalry Division
Fort Bliss, Texas
1921-1941

1st Cavalry Brigade
Fort Clark, Texas

2nd Cavalry Brigade
Fort Bliss, Texas

 5th Cavalry
Regiment
Fort Clark, TX

7th Cavalry
Regiment
Fort Bliss, TX

 12th Cavalry
Regiment
Fort Brown, TX

8th Cavalry
Regiment
Fort Bliss, TX

 82nd Field Artillery
Squadron
Fort Bliss, TX

1st Cavalry
Quartermaster
Squadron
Fort Bliss, TX

 8th Engineer
Fort McIntosh, TX

1st Cavalry Medical
Squadron
Fort Bliss, TX

First Cavalry Division

Unit 1919-1941 Location Date/s Status of unit
7 Dec 1941-
1st Cavalry HQ/HHT Fort Bliss, TX 1 Feb. 1921-
Division 1 Oct. 1941- 7 Dec. 1941

1st Cavalry HQ/HHT Demobilized 14 Jul. 1919-
Brigade Camp Harry J. Jones, AZ 1 Sep. 1921-

Fort Clark, TX 3 Feb. 1923-
Fort Bliss, TX 6 Feb. 1941- 1st Cavalry
7 Dec. 1941 Division

1st Cavalry HQ/HHT Camp Harry J. Jones, AZ June 1919-
Regiment Camp Marfa, TX 20 Aug. 1921-
Relieved from 1st Cavalry Division 3 Jan. 1933- 1st Armored
Regiment

10th Cavalry HQ/HHT Fort Huachuca, AZ Jun. 1919
Regiment Assigned to 1st Cavalry Division 20 Aug. 1921
Relieved from 1st Cavalry Division 18 Dec. 1922-

5th Cavalry HQ/HHT Fort Bliss, TX June 1919-
Regiment Camp Marfa, TX 21 Sep. 1919-
Fort Clark, TX 17 Oct. 1921
Assigned to 2nd Cavalry Division 24 Mar. 1923-
Assigned to 1st Cavalry Division 3 Jan 1933-
Fort Brown, TX 6 Feb. 1941- 1st Cavalry
Fort Bliss, TX 7 Dec. 1941 Division

12th Cavalry HQ/HHT Camp Furlong, NM June 1919-
Regiment   Camp Robert F.L. Michie, TX 11 Apr. 1921
Fort Brown, TX 6 Feb. 1941- 1st Cavalry
Fort Bliss, TX 7 Dec. 1941 Division
1st Machine HQ/HHT Camp Harry J. Jones, AZ 1 Sep. 1921-
Gun Fort Clark, TX 23 Jan 1923-
Squadron Demobilized 1 Feb 1928-

2nd Cavalry HQ/HHT Demobilized 9 Jul. 1919-
Brigade Fort Bliss, TX 14 Sep. 1921- 1st Cavalry
7 Dec. 1941 Division

7th Cavalry HQ/HHT Fort Bliss, TX June 1919-
Regiment 3rd Sqdrn Demobilized 20 Aug 1921-
1st Sqdrn Camp Marfa, TX Sep 1921-

Fort Bliss, TX 30 Jan 1923- 1st Cavalry
7 Dec. 1941 Division

8th Cavalry HQ/HHT Camp Marfa, TX Jun. 1919
Regiment Fort Bliss, TX 9 Oct 1919-
Assigned to 1st Cavalry Division 15 Sep. 1921 1st Cavalry
7 Dec. 1941 Division

2nd Machine HQ/HHT Fort Bliss, TX 26 Aug 1921-
Gun Demobilized 1 Feb 1928-
Squadron

82nd Field HQ/HHB Fort Bliss, TX Jun. 1919
Artillery Demobilized (- 1st and 2nd Bn) 9 Sep. 1921
Regiment
1st BN Redesignated 82nd FAB 9 Sep. 1921
Reactivated at Fort Bliss, TX 1 Dec 1934-
Redesignated 82nd FAB 3 Jan 1941- 1st Cavalry
Fort Bliss, TX 7 Dec. 1941 Division

8th Engineer HQ/HHCCamp Newton D. Baker, TX Jun. 1919
Squadron Fort Bliss, TX Assigned to 1st Cavalry Division 15 Sep 1921-
Fort McIntosh, TX 13 May 1928- 1st Cavalry
Fort Bliss, TX 7 Dec. 1941 Division

1st Medical HQ/HHT Fort Bliss, TX 1 Jun 1926- 1st Cavalry
Squadron 7 Dec. 1941 Division

16th Quartermaster Fort Bliss, TX 20 Sep 1921- 1st Cavalry
Squadron 7 Dec. 1941 Division

Panama Canal Division
Fort Amador, CZ
1921-1932

Panama Canal Department
Fort Amador, CZ
1932-1938

19th Infantry Brigade
Fort Davis, CZ

20th Infantry Brigade
Camp Gaillard, CZ
1922-1927

14th Infantry
Regiment
Fort Davis, CZ.

42nd Infantry Rgt.
Rio Piedras, PR

33rd Infantry
Regiment
Fort Clayton, CZ

65th Infantry Rgt.
San Juan, PR

1st Battalion
2nd Field Artillery Regiment
Fort Davis, CZ 1930-1932
Fort Clayton, CZ 1932-1938

11th Engineer
Regiment
Corozol, CZ

Panama Canal Division

Unit 1919-1941 Location Date/s Status of unit
7 Dec 1941-

Panama HQ/HHC Quarry Heights, CZ 3 Jul 1921-
Division Fort Amador, CZ Oct 1921-
Disbanded 10 Oct 1938-

19th InfantryHQ/HHC Post of Gatun, CZ 19 Mar 1921-
Brigade Fort Davis, CZ 3 Jul 1921-
Inactivated 15 Apr 1932-
Demobilized 27 Nov 1934- Demobilized

14th Infantry HQ/HHC Camp Custer, MI Jun. 1919
Regiment Fort Davis, CZ 3 Jul 1921-
Relieved from Panama Division 10 Oct 1938-
Relieved from Atlantic Sector 16 Feb 1940-
Assigned to Panama Mobile Force 16 Feb 1940-
Fort Davis, CZ 7 Dec 1941- Pan Mobile Force

33rd Infantry HQ/HHC Post of Gatun, CZ Jun. 1919
Regiment 3rd BN Camp Gaillard, CZ 11 Nov 1919-
Fort Clayton, CZ 25 Oct 1920-
Relieved from Panama Division 15 Apr 1932-
Relieved from Pacific Sector 16 Feb 1940-
Assigned to Panama Mobile Force 16 Feb 1940-
Fort Clayton, CZ 7 Dec 1941- Pan Mobile Force

20th Infantry HQ/HHC Camp Gaillard, CZ 24 Nov 1921-
Brigade Inactivated 21 Aug 1922-
Reactivated 21 Nov 1922-
Inactivated 1 Sep 1927-
Demobilized 27 Nov 1934-
42nd Infantry HQ/HHC Camp Upton, NY Jun 1919-
Regiment Camp Gaillard, CZ 10 Dec 1920-
Assigned to Panama Division 3 Jul 1922-
Inactivated - 3rd BN 30-Apr-27

42nd Infantry 3rd BN San Juan, PR 31 Jul 1927-
Regiment Inactivated - 3rd BN 31 Jul 1927-
Reorganized as an RAI Regiment 28 May 1929-
San Juan, PR 7 Dec 1941-

65th Infantry HQ/HHC San Juan, PR Jun 1919-

Regiment 1st BN Transfer to Henry Barracks, PR 31 Jul 1931-
Borinquen Field, PR 1 Feb 1940-
Fort Buchannan, PR 7 Dec 1941-
3rd BN Disbanded 31 Jul 1931-
Ft Buchannan, PR -
1st and 2nd BN 1 Feb 1940-
3rd BN Activated at Ft Buchannan, PR 1 Feb 1940-

10th Field HQ/HHB Not Organized 1930-1941- Inactive
Artillery Inactive 7 Dec 1941-
Brigade

2nd Field HQ/HHB Fort Davis, CZ 17 Mar 1930- 2nd FA
Artillery 1st BN Fort Davis, CZ 30 Mar 1930- Battalion
Regiment Assigned to Pacific Sector 15 Apr 1932-
1st BN Fort Clayton, CZ 20 Mar 1934-
Relieved from Panama Canal Div 1 Oct 1938-

11th Engineer HQ/HHC Corozol, CZ 20 Nov 1920-
Regiment Assigned to Panama Division 3 Jul 1921-
Relieved from Panama Division 10 Oct 1938-
Fort Clayton, CZ 13 Jan 1940-
Assign. to Panama Mobile Force 1 Feb 1940-
Fort Clayton, CZ   7 Dec 1941- 11th Engineer Bn.

*A Rifle Company of the 33rd Infantry Regiment
Road marching in Panama*

*14th Infantry Regiment., Panama
Division soldier
company formation on sentry duty*

Fort Davis, Panama Canal Zone

Hawaiian Division
Schofield Barracks
Territory of Hawaii
1921-1941

 21st Infantry
Brigade

22nd Infantry
Brigade

 19th Infantry
Regiment

27th Infantry
Regiment

 21st Infantry
Regiment

35th Infantry
Regiment

11th Field Artillery
Brigade
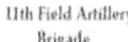

 8th Field Artillery
Regiment

3rd Engineer
Regiment

 11th Field Artillery
Regiment

11th Quartermaster
Regiment
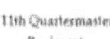

 13th Field Artillery
Regiment

11th Medical
Regiment

Hawaiian Division

Unit 1919-1941 Location Date/s Status of unit
7 Dec 1941-

Hawaiian HQ/HHC Schofield Barracks TH 1 Feb. 1921-
Division Inactivated 1 Oct. 1941-

21st Infantry HQ/HHC Schofield Barracks TH 28 Sep. 1920 Disbanded
Brigade Assigned to Hawaiian Div. 1 Mar. 1921
Disbanded 1 Oct. 1941-

19th Infantry HQ/HHC Camp Harry J. Jones, AZ Jun. 1919
Regiment Presidio of San Francisco 16 Jun 1922-
Assigned to Hawaiian Div. 17 Oct 1922-
Schofield Barracks TH 17 Oct 1922-
Assigned to 24th Division 26 Aug 1941-
7 Dec 1941- 24th Division

21st Infantry HQ/HHC Fort George Wright, WA Jun. 1919
Regiment Assigned to Hawaiian Div. 22 Oct 1921-
Schofield Barracks TH 28 Nov 1922-
Assigned to 24th Division 26 Aug 1941-
Schofield Barracks TH 7 Dec 1941- 24th Division

22nd Infantry HQ/HHC Schofield Barracks TH 16 Nov. 1921
Brigade Disbanded 1 Oct. 1941 Disbanded

27th Infantry HQ/HHC Siberia, Russia May. 1919
Regiment Manila, PI 17 Mar. 1920
Schofield Barracks TH 1 Mar. 1921
Assigned to 25th Division 26 Aug. 1941
Schofield Barracks TH 7 Dec 1941- 25th Division

35th Infantry HQ/HHC Camp Travis, TX Jun. 1919
Regiment Fort Lewis, WA 16 Nov. 1919
Schofield Barracks TH 25 Sep. 1920
Assigned to 25th Division 26 Aug. 1941
Schofield Barracks TH 7 Dec 1941- 25th Division

11th Field HQ/HHB Schofield Barracks TH 1 Mar. 1921
Artillery Redesignated 26 Aug. 1941
Brigade

24th Division Artillery 26 Aug. 1941 24th Division
Redesignated 7 Dec 1941-

8th Field HQ/HHB Camp Funston, KS 27 Jun. 1919
Artillery Presidio of San Francisco 15 Jan. 1921
Regiment Schofield Barracks TH 5 Feb. 1921
Reorganized and Redesignated 1 Oct. 1941 8th FAB
7 Dec 1941- 25th Division

11th Field HQ/HHB Camp Grant, IL 17 Jun. 1919
Artillery Presidio of San Francisco 27 Dec. 1920
Regiment Schofield Barracks TH 2 Mar. 1921
3rd BN Disbanded 1 Mar. 1940
Reorganized and Redesignated 1 Oct. 1941 11th FAB
7 Dec 1941- 24th Division

13th Field HQ/HHB Camp Dodge, IA 31 Jul. 1919
Artillery Fort Lewis, WA 22 Aug. 1920
Regiment Schofield Barracks TH 5 Feb. 1921
Reorganized and Redesignated 1 Oct. 1941 13th FAB
7 Dec 1941- 24th Division

3rd Engineer HQ/HHC Fort William Mc Kinley Jun. 1919
Regiment 2nd BN Corozol, Panama Jun. 1920
Schofield Barracks TH 5 Feb. 1921
Reorganized and Redesignated 26 Sep. 1941 3rd Eng. Bn 3rd Engineer
Battalion 7 Dec 1941- 24th Division

11th Medical HQ/HHC Schofield Barracks TH 1 Dec. 1922
Regiment   Reorganized and Redesignated 1 Oct. 1941 24th Med.

11th Quartermaster
Regiment

11th Quarter- HG/HHC Schofield Barracks, TH 3 May. 1921
master Reorganized and Redesignated 1 Oct. 1941 24th QM BN.
Regiment 24th Quartermaster Battalion 7 Dec. 1941 24th Division

Hawaiian Division Commander and Staff 1936 Schofield Barracks T.H.
Future Gen. George S. Patton in back row sixth from right

Christmas Card from Hawaii   BAR range qualifications
19th Infantry Regiment   35th Infantry Regiment

21st Infantry Regiment Band

Medical

Schofield Barracks, TH

Division,

Schofield Barracks

Members of the 11th

Regiment Hawaiian

Philippine Division
Fort McKinley
Philippine Islands
1922-1941

23rd Infantry Brigade (PS)
Fort McKinley, PI
1921-1941

24th Infantry Brigade
Manila, PI
1922-1930

45th Infantry
Regiment (PS)
Fort McKinley, PI

1st Battalion
15th Infantry Rgt.
Manila, PI
Sep.1921-Apr. 1929

57th Infantry
Regiment (PS)
Fort McKinley, PI

31st Infantry
Regiment
Manila, PI

24th Field Artillery
Regiment (PS)
Fort Stotensberg, PI

12th Quartermaster
Regiment (PS)
Fort McKinley, PI

14th Engineer
Regiment (PS)
Fort McKinley, PI

12th Medical
Regiment (PS)
Fort McKinley, PI

Philippine Division

Unit 1919-1941 Location Date/s Status of unit 7 Dec 1941-

Philippine HQ/HHC Fort McKinley, PI 10 Apr 1922-
Division 7 Dec 1941-

23rd Infantry HQ/HHC Fort McKinley, PI 5 Jan 1922-
Brigade (PS) Inactivated 19 Apr 1941- Inactive

45th Infantry HQ/HHC Camp Gordon, GA Jun. 1919
Regiment (PS) Camp Dix, NJ 4 Sep 1919-
Fort McKinley, PI 2 Dec 1920-
1st BN Camp John Hay PI 3 Dec 1920- Demobilized
2nd BN Petitt Barracks, PI 3 Dec 1920-
Assigned to Philippine Div. 22 Oct 1921-
Fort McKinley, PI 7 Dec 1941-

57th HQ/HHC Camp Pike, AR Jun. 1919
Infantry Camp Dix, NJ 11 Nov 1919-
Regiment (PS) Fort McKinley, PI 2 Dec 1920-
Assigned to Philippine Div. 22 Oct 1921-
7 Dec 1941-

24th Infantry HQ/HHC Fort Santiago, Manila, PI 26 Aug 1922-
Brigade Inactivated 26 Jun 1929- Inactive

15th HQ/HHC Jun 1919-
Infantry
Regiment 1st BN Transfer to Fort McKinley, PI Sep 1921-
Regiment -1st BN Relieved 1 Apr 1923-
from Philippine Division
1st BN Inactivated 1 Apr 1929-
Relieved from Philippine Division 26 Jun 1931-
Relieved from China Service 2-Mar 1938
7 Dec 1941- 3rd Division

31st Infantry HQ/HHC Siberia, Russia Jun 1919-
Regiment Fort McKinley, PI 16 Arp 1920
Post of Manila, PI 16 Dec 1920-
HHC/1st BN Cuartel DeEspania, Manila 16 Dec 1920-

31st 2nd/ 3rd Cuartel De Infanteria, Manila 16 Dec 1920-

Infantry Assigned to Philippine Division 22 Oct 1921-
Regiment Relieved from Philippine Div. 26 Jun 1931-
Assigned to Philippine Div. Dec 1941-
Fort McKinley, PI 7 Dec 1941-

12th Field HQ/HHB Fort McKinley, PI Jan 1922-
Artillery Inactivated 30 Sep 1922-
Brigade (PS)

24th Field HQ/HHB Fort Stotsenburg, PI 15 May 1921-
Artillery 7 Dec 1941-
Regiment (PS)

14th Engineer HQ/HHC Camp Eldridge, PI 3 May 1921-
Regiment (PS) 1stBN Disbanded 12-Sep-22
Fort McKinley, PI 22 Sep 1921-
2nd BN Assigned to Camp Mills, PI 23 Sep 1921-
Regiment Reactivated 19 Apr. 1941-
Fort McKinley, PI 7 Dec 1941-

12th Medical HQ/HHC Fort McKinley, PI 7 Dec 1921-
Regiment (PS) 7 Dec 1941-

12th Quarter- HQ/HHC Fort McKinley, PI 3 May. 1921
master 7 Dec 1941-
Regiment (PS)

Co. A, 57th Infantry Reg. (PS) 31st Infantry Regiment
Fort William McKinley, P.I. Siberia, Russia 1919-21

Mile Long Barracks, Topside YMCA Fort William McKinley
Fort Mills, Corregidor, PI Philippine Islands Regiment

26th Cavalry Regiment (PS) Soldiers of the 31st Infantry ON
Fort Stotsenberg, PI guard during the Shanghai Intervention 1932

8th Infantry Brigade
(4th Division)
Fort McPherson, GA
1922-1940

8th Infantry Regiment
Fort Moultrie, SC

22nd Infantry Regiment
Fort McPherson, GA

10th Infantry Brigade
(5th Division)
Fort Benjamin Harrison, IN
1922-1939

10th Infantry Regiment
Fort Thomas, KY

11th Infantry Regiment
Fort Benjamin Harrison, IN

12th Infantry Brigade
(6th Division)
Fort Sheridan, IL
1922-1939

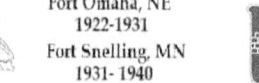

2nd Infantry Regiment
Fort Wayne, MI

6th Infantry Regiment
Jefferson Barracks, MO

14th Infantry Brigade
(7th Division)
Fort Omaha, NE
1922-1931
Fort Snelling, MN
1931- 1940

3rd Infantry Regiment
Fort Snelling, MN

17th Infantry Regiment
Fort Crook, NE

16th Infantry Brigade
(8th Division)
Washington DC
1931-1936
Fort Meade, MD
1936-1940

12th Infantry Regiment
Fort Howard, MD

34th Infantry Regiment
Fort Meade, MD

18th Infantry Brigade
(9th Division)
Army Base, Boston, MA
1931-1939
Fort William Davis, CZ
1939-1940

5th Infantry Regiment
Fort Williams, ME

13th Infantry Regiment
Fort Devens, MA

Support Regiments
US Army Infantry School
Fort Benning, GA

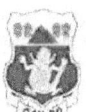

24th Infantry Regiment

29th Infantry Regiment

Separate Regiments

15th Infantry Regiment
2nd and 3rd Battlions
American Barracks, Tientsen China
1912-1938

25th Infantry Regiment
Fort Stephen Little, AZ
1919-1933
Fort Huachuca, AZ
1933-1941

THE INTERWAR ARMY
THE REGIMENT

Since the formation of the US Army, the Regiment has served as the organic combat unit. Through the years other auxiliary units were created to serve and support the Regiment. This concept is still in effect today as it would have been during the Interwar Years of the United States Army.

The Interwar years would find the Army's regimental units scattered throughout the continental US and overseas territories. Many of these units would be affiliated with a higher headquarters, a department, a division, or a brigade.

The Regiment manpower contained anywhere from 1,440 to 3320 soldiers, depending on branch or service support. Designed to operate internally as a sole unit focused on its primary mission, whatever that may have been. Externally the Regiment could be assigned or attached to a higher headquarters for the purposes of fulfilling its primary mission.

The Regiment contained a Headquarters and Headquarters Company along with assigned support units. Sub-divided into battalions for command-and-control purposes. Again, sub-divided into individual companies, squadrons, and batteries. Structure of a regiment varied from branch to branch.

With mobilization during WWI, many regiments were consolidated with a functional parent division. The Regular Army was able to organize seven full and one partial division for service in Europe. These divisions (Square Division) normally contained four Infantry regiments, three Field Artillery, and necessary support regiments or battalions.

All regiments within the Regular Army were tasked with training Organized Reserve units and personnel. National Guard units asked for assistance from their Regular counterparts for summer camp training. This would normally happen during the summer months and in the fall the Regulars would conduct their own unit training. Even though their personnel numbers may have been lower than authorized, Regular units were expected to be combat ready and available for immediate mobilization.

For many career enlisted soldiers, their branch, and most times, their regiment, was a source of great pride. Many would remain within the same organization for twenty or more years before retiring. Even with the vast scattering of the Army, soldiers rarely would transfer to other units unless they were promoted into a new position or rank, but generally within the same regiment. Those looking for adventure in exotic places may have reenlisted for an overseas assignment.

It was during WWI that Army units provincially began to design and wear a shoulder sleeve insignia (SSI) on the upper left sleeve. This was later approved by the War Department for all army units 19 October 1918.

The Department of War in 1919 organized the military heraldry program for the development of individual regimental coats of arms and distinctive unit insignia (DUI). The War Department authorized the program on 29 April 1920 (Circular 244 1921). In 1924 the program was delegated to the Quartermaster General; it is during the 1920s most of the regiments in the Army started issuing and wearing a unit crest.

Most units during the 20s had applied for and received permission to wear their units coat of arms. These distinctive insignias indicated past services in the unit's history. It also fostered pride in the soldier's unit and created a esprit de corps within the unit.

Regimental flags also began to display the unit shield, crest and the unit's motto, components of the unit's coat of arms.

The first unit to be authorized a DUI was the 51st Artillery (March 18, 1922).

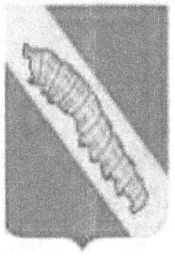

51st Field Artillery

Soldiers of the 15th Infantry Regiment pose with their Distinctive Insignia Units would not only wear the DUI on their uniforms, but could be found on Regimental flags, buildings, equipment, stationary, anything to build pride in their unit and create an esprit-de-corp amongst its soldiers.

At the heart of the US Army during the interwar years was the Infantry regiment. Army doctrine past and present was developed around the infantry branch. Field Artillery units provided indirect fire support; cavalry provided reconnaissance and other supply and support units all contributed to the success of the infantry mission.

The standard infantry regiment would require 3,106 officers and enlisted men. Commanded by a Colonel, the regiment consisted of three infantry battalions of three rifle companies, a heavy weapons company and various support elements.

Many regiments during the interwar period would not reach these numbers and many regiments were represented by only one or two undermanned battalions.

Prior to the start of the twentieth century, the US Army Infantry fielded 25 regiments, all scattered throughout the continental United States. In the aftermath of the Spanish-American War, five more regiments were added in 1901 for the newly acquired overseas garrisons. The year 1916 seven more regiments were organized for further overseas possession protection.

With the advent of America's entry into WWI, the Army organized 23 more infantry regiments for service in Europe.

The United States had committed slightly over two million men from the Army during WWI. After the war and into 1919, a force of 840,000 was still activated with many performing occupation duties in Germany.

With the passage of the National Defense Act of 1920, the Army's size was limited to 228,650 personnel. This number was never maintained during the 1920s and 1930s. Actual size wavered from 133,000 to 146,000 personnel Army wide. Among these numbers, 27 to 29 percent were stationed in overseas garrisons.

America's peacetime army had regiments spread all over the country and in overseas garrisons. The Army assumed a continental defense of the nation. Many of the infantry regiments were assigned to one of the three active Infantry Divisions in the United States; others assigned to one of the three overseas departments: while others were assigned to an inactive division or were designated as a separate regiment. Again, many regiments were cut in personnel and some set in an inactive status with a small amount of personnel.

During the Interwar Period the US Army fielded 40 infantry regiments, 12 of which were assigned to overseas stations.

USA Infantry Regiments
1919-1941

1st Infantry   2nd Infantry   3rd Infantry   4th Infantry

5th Infantry   6th Infantry   7th Infantry   8th Infantry

9th Infantry   10th Infantry   11th Infantry   12th Infantry

13th Infantry   14th Infantry   15th Infantry   16th Infantry

17th Infantry   18th Infantry   19th Infantry   20th Infantry

21st Infantry   22nd Infantry   23rd Infantry   24th Infantry

25th Infantry   26th Infantry   27th Infantry   28th Infantry

29th Infantry   30th Infantry   31st Infantry   32nd Infantry

33rd Infantry   34th Infantry   35th Infantry   36th Infantry

42nd Infantry   45th Infantry   57th Infantry   65th Infantry

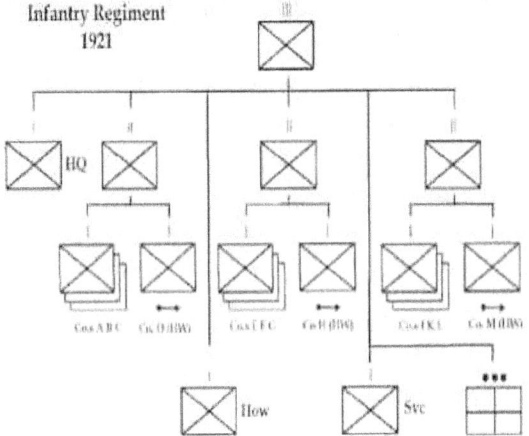

Infantry Regiment 1921

Regimental review 15th Infantry Regiment
American Barracks, Tienstin, China
US Army Infantry Regiments 1919-1941

Infantry STATION Years at location
Regiment Headquarters Location

1st Camp Lewis, Washington 1919-1921
Fort Sam Houston, Texas 1921-1927
Fort Francis E. Warren, Wyoming 1927-1940
Fort Leonard Wood, Missouri 1940-1941
2nd Camp Sherman, Ohio 1919-1922
Fort Sheridan, Illinois 1922-1929
Fort Wayne, Michigan 1929-1940
Fort Custer, Michigan 1940-1941
3rd Eagle Pass, Texas 1919-1920
Camp Sherman, Ohio 1920-1921
Fort Snelling, Minnesota 1921-1941
4th Camp Pike, Arkansas 1919-1921
Camp Lewis, Washington 1921-1922
Fort George Wright, Washington 1922-1940
Anchorage, Territory of Alaska 1940-1941
5th Fort Zachary Taylor, Kentucky 1919
Adernache, Georgia 1919-1922
Fort Williams, Maine 1922-1939
Camp Parisio, Panama Canal Zone 1939-1941
6th Camp Gordon, Georgia 1919-1920
Camp Jackson, South Carolina 1920-1921
Jefferson Barracks, Missouri 1921-1939
Fort Knox, Kentucky 1939-1941
7th Camp Pike, Arkansas 1919-1921
Camp Lewis, Washington 1921-1922
7th Vancouver Barracks, Washington 1922-1941
Fort Lewis, Washington 1941
8th Coblenz, Germany 1919-1923
Fort Screven, Georgia 1923-1929
Fort Moultrie, South Carolina 1929-1940

Fort Benning, Georgia 1940-1941
9th Fort Sam Houston, Texas 1919-1941
10th Camp Custer, Michigan 1919-1920
Camp Sherman, Ohio 1920-1921
Camp Knox, Kentucky 1921-1922
Fort Thomas, Kentucky 1922-1939
Fort McClellan, Alabama 1940
Fort Custer, Michigan 1940-1941
Iceland 1941
11th Camp Gordon, Georgia 1919-1920
Camp Jackson, South Carolina 1920-1921
Camp Knox, Kentucky 1921-1923
Fort Benjamin Harrison, Indiana 1923-1941
Fort Custer, Michigan 1941
12th Fort George C. Meade, Maryland 1919-1922
Fort Howard, Maryland 1922-1940
Arlington Cantonment, Virginia 1940-1941
Fort Dix, New Jersey 1941
Fort Benning, Georgia 1941
13th Camp Merritt, New Jersey 1919-1920
Camp Devens, Massachusetts 1920-1921
Fort Andrews, Massachusetts 1921-1922
Fort Warren, Massachusetts 1922-1925
Fort Adams, Rhode Island 1925-1928
Fort Andrews, Massachusetts 1928-1931
Fort Devens, Massachusetts 1931-1939
Fort Davis, Panama Canal Zone 1939-1940
Camp Jackson, South Carolina 1940-1941
14th Camp Custer, Michigan 1919-1920
Fort Davis, Panama Canal Zone 1920-1941
15th American Barracks, Tientsen, China 1919-1938
Fort Lewis, Washington 1938-1941
16th Camp Zachary Taylor, Kentucky 1919-1920
Camp Dix, New Jersey 1920-1922
Fort Jay, New York 1922-1939
Fort Benning, Georgia 1939-1940
Fort Jay, New York 1940-1941

Fort Devens, Massachusetts 1941
17th Fort George C. Meade, Maryland 1919-1920
Fort McIntosh, Texas 1920-1921
Fort Sam Houston, Texas 1921-1922
Fort Crook, Nebraska 1922-1940
Fort Ord, California 1940-1941
18th Camp Zachary Taylor, Kentucky 1919-1920
Camp Dix, New Jersey 1920-1922
Fort Slocum, New York 1922-1927
Fort Hamilton New York 1928-1939
Fort Benning, Georgia 1939-1940
Fort Hamilton New York 1940-1941
19th Camp Harry J. Jones, Arizona 1919-1920
Camp Sherman, Ohio 1920-1921
Presidio of San Francisco, California 1921-1922
Schofield Barracks, Territory of Hawaii 1922-1941
20th Fort Riley, Kansas 1919
Fort Crooke, Nebraska 1919-1920
Fort Sam Houston, Texas 1920-1927
Fort Francis E. Warren, Wyoming 1927-1939
Fort Jackson, South Carolina 1939-1940
Fort Benning, Georgia 1940
Fort Francis E. Warren, Wyoming 1940-1941
Fort Leonard Wood, Missouri 1941
21st Fort George Wright, Washington 1919-1921
Schofield Barracks, Territory of Hawaii 1921-1942
22nd Fort Jay, New York 1919-1922
Fort McPherson Georgia 1922-1940
Fort McClellan, Alabama 1940-1941
Fort Benning, Georgia 1941
23rd Fort Sam Houston, Texas 1919-1941
24th (Cld) Camp Furlong, New Mexico 1919-1922
Fort Benning, Georgia 1922-1941
25th (Cld) Camp Stephen D. Little, Arizona 1919-1933
Fort Huachuca, Arizona 1933-1941
26th Camp Zachary Taylor, Kentucky 1919-1920
Fort Dix, New Jersey 1920-1922

Plattsburgh Barracks, New York 1922-1941
27th Vladivostok, Siberia, Russia 1919-1920
Post of Manila, Philippine Islands 1920-1921
Schofield Barracks, Territory of Hawaii 1921-1941
28th Camp Zachary Taylor, Kentucky 1919-1920
Fort Dix, New Jersey 1920-1922
Fort Niagara, New York 1922-1941
29th Camp Shelby, Mississippi 1919
Fort Benning, Georgia 1919-1941
30th Camp Pike, Arkansas 1919-1921
Presidio of San Francisco, California 1921-1940
Fort Ord, California 1940
Presidio of San Francisco, California 1940-1941
Fort Lewis, Washington 1941
31st Vladivostok, Siberia, Russia 1919-1920
Fort McKinley, Philippine Islands 1920
Post of Manila, Philippine Islands 1920-1941
32nd Camp Kearny, California 1919-1920
Presidio of San Francisco, California 1920-1921
Los Angeles, California (ROTC cadre) 1926-1940
Fort Ord, California 1940-1941
33rd Gatun, Panama Canal Zone 1919-1920
Fort Clayton, Panama Canal Zone 1920-1941
34th Camp Funston, Kansas 1919-1921
Fort George C. Meade, Maryland 1921
Madison Barracks, New York 1921-1922
Fort Eustis, Virginia 1921-1931
Fort George C. Meade, Maryland 1931-1940
Fort Benning, Georgia 1940
35th Camp Lewis, Washington 1919-1920
Schofield Barracks, Territory of Hawaii 1920-1941
36th Inactive
37th Inactive
38th Camp Pike, Arkansas 1919-1921
Camp Lewis, Washington 1921-1922
Fort Douglas, Utah 1922-1939
Camp Bullis, Texas 1939-1941

Fort Sam Houston, Texas 1941
39th-41st Inactive
42nd (PR) Camp Upton, New York 1919-1920
Camp Gaillard, Panama Canal Zone 1920-1927
Inactive 1927-1929
42nd (PR) Rio Piedras, Puerto Rico 1929-1937
San Juan, Puerto Rico 1937-1941
43rd (PS) Camp Travis, Texas 1919
Camp Lee, Virginia 1919-1921
Fort William McKinley, Philippine Islands 1921
Fort Mills, Philippine Islands 1921-1922
Inactive 1922-1941
44th Presidio of San Francisco, California 1919-1920
Schofield Barracks, Territory of Hawaii 1921
45th (PS) Camp Gordon, Georgia 1919
Camp Dix, New Jersey 1919-1920
Fort Mason, California 1920
Fort William McKinley, Philippine Islands 1920-1941
46th-56th Inactive
57th (PS) Camp Pike, Arkansas 1919
Camp Dix, New Jersey 1919-1920
Fort William McKinley, Philippine Islands 1920-1941
62nd (PS) Camp Lee, Virginia 1919-1921
Fort Mills, Philippine Islands 1921
65th (PR) San Juan, Puerto Rico 1919-1940
Fort Buchanan, Puerto Rico 1940-1941

Future Chief of Staff Gen. George C. Marshall serving on the Infantry Board 1927 (first row, second from right)

29th Infantry Regiment Fort Benning, GA
A display and demonstration of infantry weapons

Infantry Assignments
1919-1941

Assigned
Infantry Year Infantry Infantry Corps Area/
Regiment Constituted Division Brigade Department
16th In 1861 1st 1st 2nd
18th In 1861 1st 1st 2nd
26th In 1901 1st 2nd 2nd
28th In 1901 1st 2nd 2nd

9th In 1855 2nd 3rd 8th
23rd In 1861 2nd 3rd 8th
1st In 1791 2nd 4th 7th
20th In 1861 2nd 4th 7th

4th In 1812 3rd 5th 9th
7th In 1812 3rd 5th 9th
30th In 1901 3rd 6th 9th
38th In 1917 3rd 6th 9th

8th In 1838 4th 8th 4th

22nd In 1861 4th 8th 4th
10th In 1855 5th 10th 5th
11th In 1861 5th 10th 5th

2nd In 1808 6th 12th 6th
6th In 1812 6th 12th 7th
3rd In 1784 7th 14th 7th
17th In 1861 7th 14th 7th

12th In 1861 8th 16th 3rd
34th In 1916 8th 16th 3rd
5th In 1808 9th 18th 1st
13th In 1861 9th 18th 1st
14th In 1861 Panama Canal 19th PCD
33rd In 1916 Panama Canal 19th PCD

19th In 1861 Hawaiian 21st HD
21st In 1861 Hawaiian 21st HD
27th In 1901 Hawaiian 22nd HD
35th In 1916 Hawaiian 22nd HD

31st In 1916 Manila Separate PD
15th In 1861 US Army China Separate PD
45th In (PS) 1917 Philippine 23rd PD
57th In (PS) 1917 Philippine 23rd PD

24th In (Cld) 1866 Fort Benning Separate 4th
25th In (Cld) 1866 Fort Huachuca Separate 8th
29th In 1901 Fort Benning Separate 4th
65th In (PR) 1899 Puerto Rico Separate 2nd

*31st Infantry Regiment Honor Guard 27th Infantry Regiment
Fort William McKinley, PI arriving in Vladivostok, Siberia
Shanghai Bowl on display 1936 15 August 1918*

*Fort William McKinley PI 15th Infantry range qualifications
45th Infantry Regiment (PS) Camp Burrowes, Chinwangtoa, China
37mm anti-tank training*

The Cavalry Regiment during the interwar years initially performed the same tasks as it had for one hundred years. Prior to 1921, the Cavalry regiment was for most times an independent unit covering a large geographical area of the continental US. Most of these Cavalry posts were in the west and southwest portion of the country.

The Cavalry units provided reconnaissance and security when attached to ground units. In the defense, the cavalry would provide covering fire and/or create a delay action.

The National Defense Act of 1920 was the beginnings of organizing the cavalry branch into the newly created Cavalry Divisions. The Regular Army created three cavalry divisions. The 1st Cavalry division was organized in 1921 with headquarters stationed at Fort Bliss, Texas. The 2nd and 3rd Cavalry Divisions were organized, but never truly organized as full divisions and were maintained in an inactive status.

The Cavalry regiment of 1921 contained 1,536 officers and enlisted troopers. The Cavalry regiment utilized and maintained over 1,600 horses and 130 pack mules. Commanded by a Colonel, the regiment included a Headquarters and Headquarters Company and a Service troop. Two squadrons were subordinate regimental headquarters. Each Squadron consisted of three Cavalry troops.

As the Army went into the 1930s, there was a debate over the future of the cavalry. Advocates for modernization and mechanization were at the forefront of this battle. Hard line cavalrymen still considered the horse soldier as a viable contribution to the Army, particularly for reconnaissance. Eventually concessions and changes would take place. First of which was the horse-mechanized cavalry, where horses were transported in trailers and then dismounted on site. Several units gave up their horses and were mechanized with trucks and half-tracks; this was the forerunner of the armored infantry battalion of WWII. Some regiments maintained the status as horse cavalry. Later in the 1930s, two regiments (1st and 13th) were converted to armored regiments, eventually serving in the 1st Armored Division.

There existed eighteen cavalry regiments in the US Army during the Interwar Period. Only one was stationed overseas, the 26th Cavalry located in the Philippines. The remaining (1st to the 17th) were all within the US. In the mid-twenties, two were reassigned as RAI regiments (15th and the 17th).

Most horse cavalry regiments maintained that status until America's entry into World War II. Horse Cavalry units converted to reconnaissance and target acquisition missions.

USA Cavalry Regiments
1919-1941

1st Cavalry	2nd Cavalry	3rd Cavalry	4th Cavalry
5th Cavalry	6th Cavalry	7th Cavalry	8th Cavalry
9th Cavalry	10th Cavalry	11th Cavalry	12th Cavalry
13th Cavalry	14th Cavalry	15th Cavalry	16th Cavalry
17th Cavalry	26th Cavalry		

Cavalry Regiment
1921

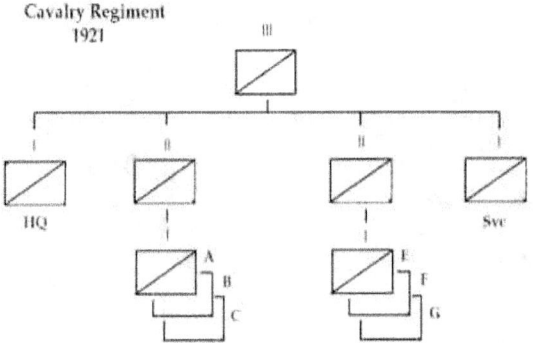

General John J. Pershing reviewing the Cavalry troop at West Point, NY

Cavalrymen utilizing Cavalry Troop on patrol, Texas

Horse-portee system Horse Cavalry troopers training
1st Cavalry Brigade with armored car unit.
(1st Cavalry Division) On maneuvers in Texas, mid 1920's

Fort Knox, KY.

Cavalry Trooper, Fort Riley, KA A Troop, 1st Cavalry Regiment
Converts to combat cars at
Fort Know, KY Early 1930's

US Army Cavalry Regiments 1919-1941

Cavalry STATION Years at location
Regiment Headquarters Location
1st Camp Harry J. Jones, Arizona 1919-1922
Camp Marfa, Texas 1923-1933
Fort Knox, Kentucky 1933-1940
2nd Fort Riley, Kansas 1919-1941
3rd Fort Myer, Virginia 1919-1941
4th Fort Ringold, Texas 1919-1920

Fort Brown, Texas 1920-1921
Fort McIntosh, Texas 1921-1924
Fort D.A. Russell, Wyoming 1924-1927
Fort Meade, South Dakota 1927-1941
5th Camp Marfa, Texas 1919-1921
Fort Clark, Texas 1921-1941
6th Fort Oglethorpe, Tennessee 1919-1941
7th Fort Bliss, Texas 1919-1941
8th Fort Bliss, Texas 1919-1941
9th (Cld) Fort Stotsenburg, Philippine Islands 1919-1922
Fort Riley, Kansas 1922-1941
10th (Cld) Fort Huachuca, Arizona 1919-1931
Fort Leavenworth, Kansas 1931-1941
11th Presidio of Monterey, California 1919-1941
12th Camp Furlong, New Mexico 1919-1920
Camp Robert F. L. Michie, Texas 1920-1921
Fort Brown, Texas 1921-1941
13th Fort Clark, Texas 1919-1920
Fort D.A. Russell, Wyoming 1920-1927
Fort Riley, Kansas 1927-1936
Fort Knox, Kentucky 1936-1941
14th Fort Sam Houston, Texas 1919-1920
Fort Des Moines, Iowa 1920-1940
Fort Riley, Kansas 1940-1941
15th Fort D.A. Russell, Wyoming 1919-1921
` 16th Fort Brown, Texas 1919-1920
Fort Sam Houston, Texas 1920-1921
Fort Myer, Virginia 1926-1938
17th Schofield Barracks, Territory of Hawaii 1919-1921
Presidio of Monterey, California 1921
26th (PS) Fort Stotsenburg, Philippine Islands 1922-1941

Cavalry Assignments 1919-1941

Cavalry Year Division Brigade
Regiment Constituted
1st 1833 1st (1921-1933) 7th (1933-1940)

2nd 1836 2nd (1919-1941) 3rd (1927-1940)
3rd 1846 3rd (1919-1941) 6th (1927-1940)
4th 1855 2nd (1923-1933) (36-41) 7th (1933-1936)
5th 1855 1st (1922-1941) 1st (1923-1941)
6th 1855 3rd (1927-1939) 6th (1927-1939)
7th 1866 1st (1921-1941) 2nd (1921-1941)
8th 1866 1st (1921-1941) 2nd (1921-1941)
9th 1866 3rd (1933-1940) 5th (1933-1940)
10th 1866 2nd (1923-1927) 3rd (1923-1927)
10th 3rd (1927-1940) 5th (1927-1940)
11th 1901 3rd (1927-1933) 5th (1927-1933)
11th 2nd (1933-1940) 4th (1933-1940)
12th 1901 2nd (1923-1933) 4th (1923-1933)
12th 1st (1933-1941) 1st (1933-1941)
13th 1901 2nd (1923-1927) (32-36) 7th (1936-1940)
14th 1901 2nd (1927-1940) 4th (1927-1940)
15th 1901 Separate RAI (1927)
16th Separate RAI (1926)
17th 1916 Separate RAI (1927)
26th 1922 Separate (1922-1941) Philippine Division

During the Interwar Period, the US Army had 33 Field Artillery regiments assigned. Only twenty were active in the Regular Army. The remaining regiments were activated as RAI (Regular Army Inactive). The regiment provided a base for artillery organizations, containing two battalions, each with three firing batteries of four guns. It must be noted that only twelve FA regiments managed to maintain a Regimental headquarters during this period. Most regiments were not totally active, where only one battalion of the regiment may be active with no regimental base.

Artillery units were assigned to Field Artillery Brigades. Many made up the artillery in divisions; others were assigned to GHQ (General Headquarters). Brigades typically included two 75mm regiments and one 155mm regiment.

The American Army during WWI placed a great deal of responsibility upon Field Artillery units. The war on the Western Front was locked into trench warfare with strong defensive positions. The Field Artillery units provided indirect fire support for ground forces. Many lessons were learned by American artillerymen. Taking what they had learned from the war aided in contributing to the development of the Interwar Field Artillery regiments.

Upon return from Europe field artillery units remained organized in a Field Artillery Brigade. The American division contained three artillery regiments, two light and one heavy. During the Interwar Period, the 155mm regiment was assigned to GHQ in Field Artillery Brigades. The two 75mm remained assigned to their parent divisions. During the Interwar Period, there were five active FA Brigades, four assigned to Regular divisions and one separate brigade, the 13th FA Brigade.

The Field Artillery Brigades (FAB) assigned to GHQ would provide the heavy guns, 155mm and 240mm regiments. Of the three FA Brigades, only the 13th FA Brigade was active, located at Fort Bragg, NC.

Many innovative improvements in weapons and fire direction centers were implemented by artillery units during this period. Training was always a priority for all interwar period units. The Field Artillery did suffer in live fire exercises since ammunition for artillery was scarce due to budgeting constraints.

Prime movers, such as tractors and/or trucks, were introduced into the Heavy (155mm) regiments in the 20s and 30s. This enhanced the movement of heavy regiments and brigades. The two division artillery regiments still employed horses and caissons up until the mid-nineteen thirties. The regiment normally contained over 1500 horses and mules.

Regular Field Artillery units also conducted annual training for their Reserve units in their Corp Area.

Field Artillery Brigade, Medium and Heavy GHQR, 1921

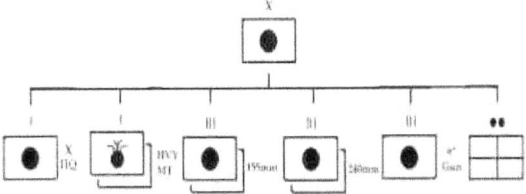

Field Artillery Brigade, Infantry Division, 1921

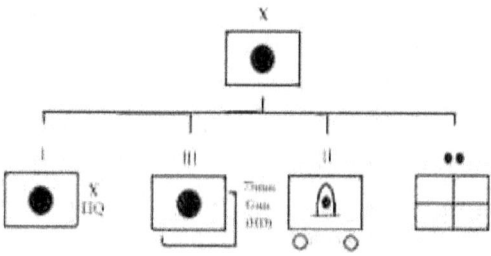

Field Artillery Regiment, 75-mm Gun, Horse Drawn, 1921

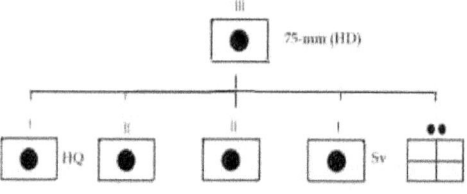

US Army Field Artillery Regiments
1919-1941

1st Field
Artillery

2nd Field
Artillery

3rd Field
Artillery

4th Field
Artillery

5th Field
Artillery

6th Field
Artillery

7th Field
Artillery

8th Field
Artillery

9th Field
Artillery

10th Field
Artillery

11th Field
Artillery

12th Field
Artillery

13th Field
Artillery

14th Field
Artillery

15th Field
Artillery

16th Field
Artillery

17th Field
Artillery

18th Field
Artillery

19th Field
Artillery

20th Field
Artillery

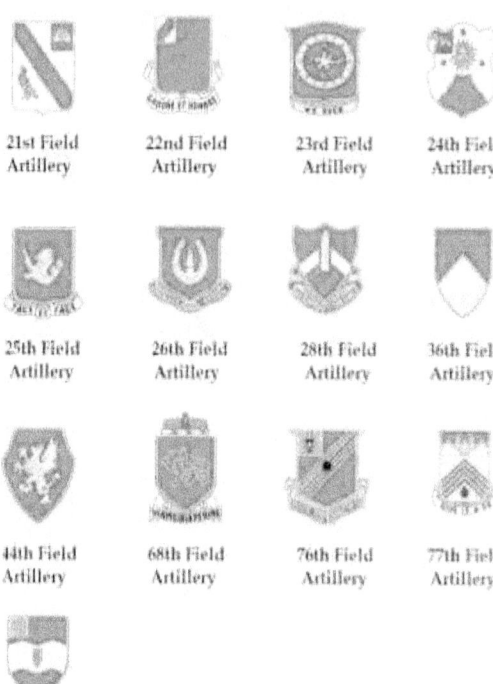

21st Field Artillery	22nd Field Artillery	23rd Field Artillery	24th Field Artillery
25th Field Artillery	26th Field Artillery	28th Field Artillery	36th Field Artillery
44th Field Artillery	68th Field Artillery	76th Field Artillery	77th Field Artillery
82nd Field Artillery			

US Army Field Artillery Regiments 1919-1941

Field STATION Years at location
Artillery Headquarters Location
Regiment

1st Fort Sill, Oklahoma 1919-1941
2nd Camp Zachary Taylor, Kentucky 1919-1920
Camp Knox, Kentucky 1920-1921
Camp Bragg, North Carolina 1921-1922
3rd Camp Grant, Illinois 1919-1921
Camp Knox, Kentucky 1921-1922
Fort McIntosh, Texas 1927-1928

Camp Knox, Kentucky 1928-1929
Fort Sheridan, Illinois 1929-1930
4th Camp Stanley, Texas 1919-1922
Fort Sam Houston, Texas 1922-1924
Fort McIntosh, Texas 1924-1927
Fort Bragg, North Carolina 1940-1941
5th Camp Zachary Taylor, Kentucky 1919-1920
Camp Bragg, North Carolina 1920-1931
Madison Barracks, New York 1931-1940
6th Camp Zachary Taylor, Kentucky 1919-1920
Camp Dix, New Jersey 1920-1922
Fort Hoyle, Maryland 1922-1940
7th Camp Zachary Taylor, Kentucky 1919-1920
Camp Dix, New Jersey 1920-1922
Fort Ethan Allen, Vermont 1922-1940
8th Camp Funston, Kansas 1919-1920
Camp George G. Meade, Maryland 1919-1921
Schofield Barracks, Territory of Hawaii 1921-1941
9th Fort Sill, Oklahoma 1919-1921
10th Camp Pike, Arkansas 1919-1921
Fort Lewis, Washington 1921-1940
11th Camp Grant, Illinois 1919-1921
Schofield Barracks, Territory of Hawaii 1921-1941
12th Camp Travis, Texas 1919-1920
Fort Sam Houston, Texas 1920-1940
13th Camp Dodge, Iowa 1919-1920
Camp Lewis, Washington 1920
Schofield Barracks, Territory of Hawaii 1920-1941
14th Fort Sill, Oklahoma 1919-1921
15th Camp Travis, Texas 1919-1920
Fort Sam Houston, Texas 1920-1929
Fort Sam Houston, Texas 1934-1940
16th Camp Lewis, Washington 1921
17th Camp Travis, Texas 1919-1920
Fort Sam Houston, Texas 1920-1921
Camp Bragg, North Carolina 1922-1941
18th Camp Pike, Arkansas 1919-1922

Fort Sill, Oklahoma 1935-1941
19th Camp Bragg, North Carolina 1919-1920
Fort Knox, Kentucky 1939-1940
20th Camp Bragg, North Carolina 1919-1920
Fort Benning, Georgia 1940
21st Camp Bragg, North Carolina 1919-1921
Fort Knox, Kentucky 1939-1940
22nd Fort Bragg, North Carolina 1927-1930
23rd Fort Bragg, North Carolina 1926-193024th (PS) Fort Stotsenburg, Philippine Islands 1921-1941
25th (PS) Fort William McKinley, Philippine Islands 1921
26th Fort Bragg, North Carolina 1940
27th Inactive
28th Camp Jackson, South Carolina 1940
29th Fort Bragg, North Carolina 1927-1940
Fort Benning, Georgia 1940
30th Camp Roberts, California 1941
31st Fort Sill, Oklahoma 1929-1933
Fort Ord, California 1940
32nd Inactive
33rd Inactive
34th Fort Bragg, North Carolina 1940-1941
35th Camp Blanding, Florida 1941
36th Fort Bragg, North Carolina 1939-1941
37th-39th Inactive
40th Camp Roberts, California 1941
41st-43rd Inactive
44th Fort Bragg, North Carolina 1941
45th Inactive
46th Inactive
47th Fort Bragg, North Carolina 1941
48th-65th Inactive
66th Camp Pine, New York 1941
67th Inactive
68th Fort Knox, Kentucky 1940-1941
69th Inactive
70th Inactive

72nd Fort Bragg, North Carolina 1941
73rd-75th Inactive
76th Camp Pike, Arkansas 1919-1921
Camp Lewis, Washington 1921-1922
Fort D. A. Russell, Wyoming 1922-1940
Presidio of Monterey, California 1940-1941
77th Camp Dodge, Iowa 1919-1920
Camp Lewis, Washington 1920-1921
Fort Bragg, North Carolina 1930-1935
Fort D. A. Russell, Wyoming 1935-1941
78th Camp Grant, Illinois 1919-1921
79th Camp Funston, Kansas 1919-1921
Camp George G. Meade, Maryland 1921
Camp Knox, Kentucky 1919-1922
80th Camp Funston, Kansas 1919-1920
Camp George G. Meade, Maryland 1920-1921
Fort Bragg, North Carolina 1927-1930
Fort Lewis, Washington 1939-1940
Fort Des Moines, Iowa 1940
81st Camp Knox, Kentucky 1919-1922
Camp Bragg, North Carolina 1922
Fort Bragg, North Carolina 1927-1930
Fort Lewis, Washington 1940
82nd Fort Bliss, Texas 1919-1921
Fort Bliss, Texas 1934-1941
83rd Camp Knox, Kentucky 1919-1921
Camp Bragg, North Carolina 1921-1922
Fort Benning, Georgia 1940-1941
84th-87th Inactive
88th Fort Stotsenburg, Philippine Islands 1941
89th-94th Inactive
99th Inactive
100th Inactive

Field Artillery
Assignments 1919-1941

Field Assigned
Artillery Year FA Corp Area/
Regiment Constituted Division Brigade Department

6th FA 1907 1st 1st 2nd
7th FA 1916 1st 1st 2nd
12th FA 1916 2nd 2nd 8th
15th FA 1917 2nd 2nd 8th
10th FA 1916 3rd 3rd 9th
76th FA 1916 3rd 3rd 9th
82nd FA 1916 1st Cav none 8th
8th FA 1916 Hawaiian 11th Hawaii
11th FA 1916 Hawaiian 11th Hawaii
13th FA 1916 Hawaiian 11th Hawaii
24th FA 1920 Philippine none Philippine
2nd FA 1907 Panama none Panama
1st FA 1907 Separate none 8th
3rd FA 1907 6th none inactive
4th FA 1907 Separate none inactive
5th FA 1907 Separate 13th FAB 2nd /4th
9th FA 1916 7th none 7th
14th FA 1916 6th none 6th
16th FA 1916 8th none 3rd
17th FA 1916 Separate 13th FAB 4th
18th FA 1916 9th inactive
19th FA 1916 5th inactive
20th FA 1916 5th inactive
21st FA 1916 5th inactive
22nd FA 1918 13th FAB inactive
23rd FA 1921 inactive
25th FA 1918 Philippine inactive
26th FA 1918 14th FAB inactive
28th FA 1918 14th FAB inactive
36th FA 1918 13th FAB inactive

44th FA 1933 17th FAB inactive
68th FA 1933 24th FAB inactive
77th FA 1916 4th none 4th /7th /8th

A Field Artillery horse drawn battery
Fort Sam Houston, TX

Field Artillery Battery (75mm) 2nd Bn, 3rd Field
Artillery
preparing to fire.   Fort Sheridan, IL.

Artillery of the 1st Battalion, 2nd FA Regiment

Experiment with air-transportation a 75mm cannon
Rio Hato, Panama 1930's

THE INTERWAR ARMY
THE COAST ARTILLERY REGIMENT

Coast artillery forts had been established back in the Revolutionary times. From that time on, the US Army had created coast artillery emplacements for America's vital ports. Through the years, as Americas foreign trade expanded, US ports were vital to this country's existence and required protection. Used as a stop gap for any foreign invader, coast artillery forts and emplacements protected America's shores for over a hundred and fifty years prior to the onset of the Interwar Army.

Throughout the years, more forts were built as the American boundaries and population grew. These mighty forts gave Americans a sense of relief from foreign invaders. The establishment of these defenses also created a great deterrent to any major power. This method of defense was very costly, yet proved its worth maintaining very positive results.

The Coast Artillery Corp was established in 1924. Prior to this time the Coast Artillery and the Field Artillery regiments had all been part of the Field Artillery. Many CAC regiments spent time on the Western Front during WWI, firing the massive artillery weapons (some dismantled from their batteries stateside and shipped to France) to provide heavy indirect fire support.

Coast Artillery regiments were assigned to a Corp Area and a Coast Artillery District. The district would include the harbors and regiments manning them. Regiments many times were distributed to different forts and batteries within their harbor defenses.

Weapon systems varied from battery to battery. Some housed the large 12-inch gun with disappearing carriages to large mortar pits, some with up to six mortars. Coast artillery soldiers tended to be more technical and acquired special skills; this led to higher pay for enlisted soldiers.

World War I introduced the airplane as an offensive weapon. The US Army initiated anti- aircraft (AA) batteries and later regiments to the Coast Artillery. Most of these AA regiments were stationed at vital centers of population (near and around large American cities), strategic centers, and CAC harbor defense networks.

The 1920s and 30s would see a major downsizing for Coast Artillery regiments and their installations. America felt safe from foreign invasion after World War I and being an isolationist nation, funding for such an expensive defense system was cut back.

Most CAC installations had consolidated its resources, which saw the closure of many batteries within harbor districts. Some installations went into caretaker status until 1939-40.

Technology also played a hand in harbor defenses. Many installations contained obsolete guns and equipment. Larger caliber guns were developed and parceled to key Coast Artillery units and emplacements. Fire direction centers gained newer and more modern equipment to accomplish that task.

During the Interwar Period, the Army committed 29 CAC regiments for harbor defense for overseas possessions and the continental United States. With the pre-mobilization in 1939-40, many vital stations were brought back to war time strength.

Coast Artillery Regiment, Tractor Drawn (TD) 155mm, 1927

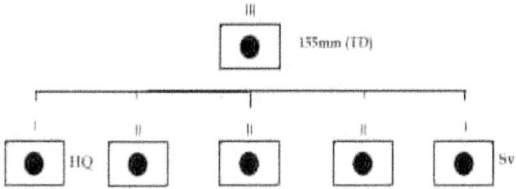

Coast Artillery Regiment, Railway (Rwy), 1921
12", 14", 16" Guns

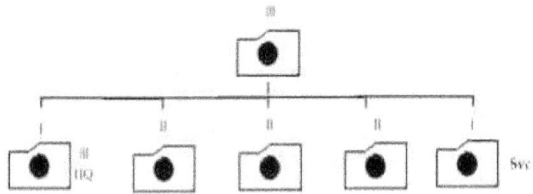

Coast Artillery Regiment, Anti-Aircraft (AA), 1930

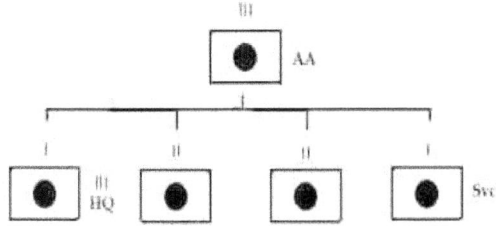

US Army Coast Artillery Regiments
1919-1941

1st Coast
Artillery (HD)

2nd Coast
Artillery (HD)

3rd Coast
Artillery (HD)

4th Coast
Artillery (HD)

5th Coast
Artillery (HD)

6th Coast
Artillery (HD)

7th Coast
Artillery (HD)

8th Coast
Artillery (HD)

9th Coast
Artillery (HD)

10th Coast
Artillery (HD)

11th Coast
Artillery (HD)

12th Coast
Artillery (HD)

13th Coast
Artillery (HD)

14th Coast
Artillery (HD)

15th Coast
Artillery (HD)

16th Coast
Artillery (HD)

41st Coast
Artillery (RY)

44th Coast
Artillery (HT)

51st Coast
Artillery (HT)

52nd Coast
Artillery (RY)

59th Coast
Artillery (HT)

60th Coast
Artillery (AA)

61st Coast
Artillery (AA)

62nd Coast
Artillery (AA)

63rd Coast
Artillery (AA)

64th Coast
Artillery (AA)

65th Coast
Artillery (AA)

91st Coast
Artillery (AA)

92nd Coast
Artillery (AA)

US Army Coast Artillery Regiments 1919-1941

Coast Artillery STATION Years at location
Regiment Headquarters Location

1st HD Fort DeLesseps, Panama Canal Zone 1924-1932
Fort Sherman, Panama Canal Zone 1932-1941
2nd HD Fort Sherman, Panama Canal Zone 1924-1932
Fort Monroe, Virginia 1932-1941

3rd HD Fort MacArthur, California 1924-1941
4th HD Fort Amador, Panama Canal Zone 1924-1941
5th HD Fort Hamilton, New York 1924-1941
6th HD Fort Winfield Scott, California 1924-1941
7th HD Fort Hancock, New Jersey 1924-1941
8th HD Fort Preble, Maine 1924-1941
9th HD Fort Banks, Massachusetts 1924-1941
10th HD Fort Adams, Rhode Island 1924-1941
11th HD Fort H.G. Wright, New York 1924-1941
12th HD Fort Monroe, Virginia 1924-1932
13th HD Fort Barrancas, Florida 1924-1941
14th HD Fort Worden, Washington 1924-1941
15th HD Fort Kamehameha, Territory of Hawaii 1924-1941
16th HD Fort DeRussey, Territory of Hawaii 1924-1927
Fort Ruger, Territory of Hawaii 1927-1941
18th HD Fort Stevens, Oregon 1940-1941
19th HD Fort Rosecrans, California 1940-1941
20th HD Fort Crockett, Texas 1940-1941
21st HD Fort DuPont, Delaware 1940-1941
22nd HD Fort Constitution, New Hampshire 1940-1941
23rd HD Fort Rodman, Massachusetts 1940-1941
41st RW Fort Kamehameha, Territory of Hawaii 1921-1931
42nd RW Camp Eustis, Virginia 1919-1921
Camp Eustis, Virginia 1926-1941
43rd RW Camp Eustis, Virginia 1919-1921
44th HT Fort Totten, New York 1919-1920
Camp Jackson, South Carolina 1920-1921
Camp Eustis, Virginia 1926-1930
51st HT Fort Hamilton, New York 1919-1920
Camp Jackson, South Carolina 1920-1921
Fort Eustis, Virginia 1921-1930
52nd RW Fort Hancock, New Jersey 1930-1941
53rd RW Fort Eustis, Virginia 1919-1921
FortEustis, Virginia 1927-1931
54th (155) Fort Totten, New York 1919-1920
Camp Jackson, South Carolina 1920-1921
Camp Wallace, Texas 1941

Camp Davis, North Carolina 1941
55th HT Camp Terry, New York 1919
Fort Winfield Scott, California 1919
Camp Lewis, Washington 1919-1921
Fort Kamehameha, Territory of Hawaii 1921-1931
56th HT Camp Jackson, South Carolina 1919-1921
57th HT Fort Winfield Scott, California 1919
Camp Lewis, Washington 1919-1921
Fort Monroe, Virginia 1941
59th HT Fort Winfield Scott, California 1919
Camp Lewis, Washington 1919-1921
Fort Mills, Philippine Islands 1921-1941
60th AA Fort Crockett, Texas 1922-1923
Fort William McKinley, Philippine Islands 1923-1929
Fort Mills, Philippine Islands 1929-1941
61st AA Fort Monroe, Virginia 1921-1930
Fort Sheridan, Illinois 1930-1941
62nd AA Fort Totten, New York 1921-1941
63rd AA Fort Winfield Scott, California 1921-1930
Fort MacArthur, California 1930-1941
64th AA Fort Shafter, Territory of Hawaii 1921-1941
65th AA Fort Amador, Panama Canal Zone 1924-1932
Fort Winfield Scott, California 1938-1941
Camp Haan, California 1941
66th AA Camp Upton, New York 1919
67th AA Presidio of San Francisco, California 1919
Fort Bragg, North Carolina 1941
68th AA Fort Wadsworth, New York 1919
Fort Williams, Maine 1939-1940
Camp Edwards, Massachusetts 1940-1941
69th AA Fort Eustis, Virginia 1919
Fort Eustis, Virginia 1927-1930
Fort McClellan, Alabama 1930-1935
Fort Crocket, Texas 1935-1941
Camp Hulen, Texas 1941
70th AA Fort Monroe, Virginia 1939-1940
Fort Moultrie, South Carolina 1940-1941

71st AA Fort Story, Virginia 1941
72nd AA Fort Randolph, Panama Canal Zone 1939-1941

Coast Artillery Assignments1919-1941

Coast Assigned
Artillery Year Corp Area/
Regiment Constituted Harbor Defense/ Brigade Department

1st HD 1924 Cristobal PCZ Panama
2nd HD 1924 Cristobal PCZ Panama
3rd HD 1924 Los Angeles / San Diego/ Columbia 9th
4th HD 1924 Balboa PCZ Panama
5th HD 1924 Southern New York 2nd
6th HD 1924 San Francisco 9th
7th HD 1924 Delaware/ Sandy Hook 2nd
8th HD 1924 Portland/ Portsmouth 1st
9th HD 1924 Boston 1st
10th HD 1924 Narragansett Bay/New Bedford 1st
11th HD 1924 Long Island Sound 1st
12th HD 1924 Potomac/ Chesapeake Bay 3rd
13th HD 1924 Charleston/ Key West/ Pensacola 4th
14th HD 1924 Puget Sound 9th
15th HD 1924 Pearl Harbor Hawaii
16th HD 1924 Honolulu Hawaii
41st RY 1924 Pearl Harbor Hawaii
44th HT 1924 39th Coast Artillery Brigade inactive
51st HT 1924 39th Coat Artillery Brigade inactive
52nd RY 1924 30th Coast Artillery Brigade 2nd/ 3rd
55th HT 1924 Honolulu Hawaii/inactive
56th HT 1917 39th Coast Artillery Brigade 4th
57th HT 1917 31st Coast Artillery Brigade inactive/ 9th
59th HT 1917 Manila and Subic Bay Philippine
60th AA 1922 Fort William McKinley, PI Philippine
61st AA 1922 Chesapeake Bay 3rd
62nd AA 1921 Eastern New York 2nd

63rd AA 1921 Los Angeles 9th
64th AA 1921 Fort Shafter Hawaii
65th AA 1924 Balboa Panama
67th AA 1926 inactive
68th AA 1926 inactive
78th AA 1923 Fort MacArthur, CA 9th
91st HD 1924 Manila and Subic Bay Philippine
92nd HD 1924 Manila and Subic Bay Philippine

AA Anti-Aircraft
HD Harbor Defense
HT Heavy/Tractor
RY Railway

Coast Artillery mortar pit   *Anti-aircraft gunnery training*

Officers of the 59th Coast Artillery Regiment
Fort Mills (Corregidor) Philippines 1930s

10" Gun w/disappearing Carriage Battery Hearn, Fort Mills, Corregidor P.I.
Fort Casey, Puget Sound, WA.

US Army Coast Artillery Districts

1st Coast Artillery
District

2nd Coast Artillery
District

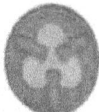

3rd Coast Artillery
District

4th Coast Artillery
District

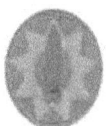

9th Coast Artillery
District

Hawaiian
Coast Artillery
Brigade

Coast Artillery Districts 1919-1941

Coast Assigned
Artillery Year Corps Area/
District Constituted Subordinate Commands Department

1st CAD 1920 Harbor Defenses of Boston 1st
Harbor Defenses of Long Island Sound 1st
Harbor Defenses of Narragansett Bay 1st

Harbor Defenses of New Bedford 1st
Harbor Defenses of Portland 1st
Harbor Defenses of Portsmouth 1st

2nd CAD 1920 Harbor Defenses of the Delaware 2nd
Harbor Defenses of Eastern New York 2nd
Harbor Defenses of Sandy Hook 2nd
Harbor Defenses of Southern New York 2nd

3rd CAD 1920 Defenses of Baltimore 3rd
Harbor Defenses of Chesapeake Bay 3rd

4th CAD 1920 Harbor Defenses of Cape Fear 4th
Harbor Defenses of Charleston 4th
Harbor Defenses of Savannah 4th
Harbor Defenses of Key West 4th
Harbor Defenses of Mobile 4th
Harbor Defenses of Pensacola 4th
Harbor Defenses of New Orleans 4th
9th CAD 1920 Harbor Defenses of Puget Sound 9th
Harbor Defenses of the Columbia 9th
Harbor Defenses of San Francisco 9th
Harbor Defenses of Los Angeles 9th
Harbor Defenses of San Diego 9th
Hawaiian 1921 Harbor Defenses of Honolulu and Hawaii
CAD Pearl Harbor
Panama Harbor Defenses of Balboa
CAD Harbor Defenses of Cristobel
Philippine Harbor Defenses of Manila and Subic Bays Philippine

The officer corps of the US Army Interwar period was a combination of the Old Army officer and the younger up and coming officer. Many of the General and field grade officers had been a factor in the Army going back to the Spanish American War, with some even to the Indian Wars. It was, however, the officers of the twentieth century that endured the Interwar the longest and made the most sacrifices to their careers. Prior to the World War, many of these junior officers would gain experience fighting in the Philippine Insurrection or been a part of the Mexican border expeditions. Further experience would be gained when America entered WWI. Most received temporary promotions and a higher command than was expected of their current pay grade. Some found their way into important staff positions that would help them in the next great war.

When the war to end wars was over, the younger officers reverted back to their permanent rank to serve the next twenty years in a peacetime army waiting on promotions and assignments.

Promotions were slow for these officers and the challenges were many. The officer corps was a transient portion of the army; officers rotated to new units and/or assignments. Junior grade officers typically could spend three to four years at a station, where senior officers were more mobile depending on assignment. The interwar officer would see a lot of the United States plus overseas assignments to China, Panama, the Philippines, Hawaii, and Alaska. Families were permitted to travel with them at the expense of the government. The Army had its own transport system for overseas garrisons. The United States Army Transport Service (USATS) provided transoceanic transport during its forty years of operation.

A major benefit to the officer corps during this period was individual professional education. Branch schools were helpful with the latest doctrine and weapons; staff training was available for consolidation of larger platforms of warfare. This training would reap tremendous benefits to the army when mobilization began for the Second World War.

ELIHU ROOT

The roots of the interwar army may have begun under the stewardship of Elihu Root as Secretary of War (1899-1904). During his tenure as Secretary, Root made many improvements in the War Department. His foresight allowed him to make some significant changes to the US Army.

In order to make the US Army more professional, he created educational stepping stones for the Army's Officer Corp. Professional development was initiated throughout the Army, beginning with Branch schools for younger officers to hone their skills. West Point was enlarged to receive new candidates for the officer corp. The Army War College was introduced during this time also. Officers were obliged to rotate from line positions to staff positions and back again to line position. This practice allowed officers of all grades to have an opportunity to see how they operate in both environments.

Also, under Root's tenure, the US Army General Staff was created. The first Chief of Staff MG Samuel Baldwin Marks Young was appointed in August 1903.

The Interwar Period provided education, training and professional development for future officer leadership for WWII.

Captain Dwight D. Eisenhower 2LT Alexander Nininger
Fort Meade, Maryland 1922 57th Infantry Regiment (PS)
34th President of the United States First Soldier in WWII to receive the

Medal of Honor (posthumously)
Abucay, Bataan, PI 12 Jan 1942

Company officers gather for morning   *Pay day activities Fort Sherman*
CZ
  formation Fort Lewis, Washington   *14th Infantry Regiment*

THE INTERWAR ARMY
THE ENLISTED SOLDIER

"The Old Army Regular had been a long-service soldier who found both a job and a permanent home in the ranks."

It should be noted that most Americans considered soldiering an ignoble profession. Most civilians kept their distance from any military installation and its personnel.

The American enlisted soldier during the Interwar years was of a varied lot. They came from many places within the US and its possessions. Most were one-termers; others stayed for several reenlistments. Most were uneducated and came from low economic backgrounds. Twelve percent were foreign born, predominately Irish, German, lastly Russian.

Soldiers served their time in all types of climes, locales, conditions, and threats. Many units served in very remote areas of the US and its possessions.

Training was imperative in the soldier's daily military life. Soldiers trained six days a week in the morning hours, with afternoons set aside for fatigue duty within their unit. Soldiers passed their skills to reserve units whom they supported at summer encampments within their Corp Area.

The noncommissioned officer (NCO) was the backbone of the unit's discipline, training, health, and welfare of their assigned soldiers. NCOs were professionals, many with many years of service as well as some with combat experience.

The Army did its best to provide care and welfare for its soldiers. Different programs for education were initiated for individual education advancement. Athletics also provided morale and a created a esprit de corps amongst the enlisted ranks. Perhaps the only detriment for soldiers was during the Prohibition era when the beer and whiskey was unavailable.

Enlistments increased during the Great Depression due to lack of gainful employment in America during this time. A new variety of enlisted men started filling the ranks of the Army. Enlistees came from all walks of life, some well-educated, or least educated, and many possessing all types of civilian skills.

In 1939, the United States Army implemented a mobilization and expansion program. Inactive and new units were brought up to strength with enlistees and conscripts. Active Regular Army units participated by providing officer and enlisted cadres for the new units being activated and mobilized. This is where the professionalism and experience of the Interwar soldier was greatly used and appreciated.

Assigned as cadre, the Regular soldiers passed their knowledge and skills to new volunteers and inductees (Selective Training and Service Act 1940). Many of these cadre soldiers would remain with the unit they trained and serve with them during WWII.

With the advent of pre-mobilization and eventually America's entry into World War II, the old garrison Army was gone. The Interwar years slipped by with many making sacrifices for the nineteenth largest Army in the world. However, post WWII would find America's military unsurpassed by any world power. This could not have been accomplished if not for the dedication to all of those Inter War officers, NCOs, and enlisted men.

25th Infantry Regiment (Cld) Fort Huachuca, AZ

Enlisted Mans Dress Uniform   Soldiers on Kitchen Patrol (KP)
1920s and 1930s   pose for picture

Pineapple   Express   transporting soldiers   Soldiers clean up after chow.

Many units on pass from Schofield Barracks to in the 1920s Honolulu, Hawaii lived in tent encampments.

THE INTERWAR ARMY
SUMMATION

For American military historians and buffs, the Interwar Period was an empty void in America's military history. The time between the world wars was passed over in so many narratives of units and their activities in the two decades between the World wars.

In the world of the 1920s and 1930s, the United States Army, a professional army, accomplished its mission, with dedication to service. Soldiers of the interwar years would overcome many hardships and disappointments. Although it had been ranked as the nineteenth in size amongst other nations, the army fulfilled extraordinary feats to maintain peace and neutrality for the United States.

Overseas garrisons were maintained and expanded during this twenty-year span, particularly Hawaii, here the garrison continually grew. America's Far East garrisons in China and the Philippines were always under the threat of a confrontation with Japanese troops, creating an uneasy situation. "Americas first cold war?" While the US Army went through several transitions during the Inter-War period it did serve as a deterrent to Japanese aggression in the Far East.

The Army within the Continental United States, although understrength, accomplished many worthy tasks, in support of the US population. During the Great Depression, the Army was tasked with administrative and implementation of the Civilian Conservation Corp {CCC} in 1932.

Events in Europe and China in the late 1930's would create concern for America's military services; however, America was still a staunch isolationist nation. Political events would call for a subliminal increase in America's readiness for eventuality of being drawn into a conflict somewhere.

Pre-mobilization plans were accomplished between 1939-1941. The Selective Service Act was passed, and America's first peace time draft begins. Eighteen National Guard Divisions were called into service for one year, beginning in September 1940.

General Headquarters (GHQ) Maneuvers of 1940 and 1941 will see the largest ever gathering of US Army units for Army versus Army wargaming.

Change was slow for the Army during the Interwar years; however, it would reap its rewards in the future. A professional Officer Corp was the greatest of its accomplishments. Along with professional NCO's, the Army had the seeds for success, as would be seen in the future.

Development of new technologies, weapons, tactics, training, and development of combat units' divisions, corps, and later establishment of armies.

The years between 1919-1941 would be the child of the United States Army. From nineteenth in size of armies of the period to the number one military presence created to engage in World War II.

Abbreviations

AA Anti-aircraft NG National Guard
B Brigade NGI National Guard Installation
Bn Battalion OC Ordinance Center
CAC Coast Artillery Corp OR Organized Reserve
ORTC Organized Reserve
Training Center
Cav Cavalry
Cld Colored PI Philippine Islands
CMTC Civilian Military Training Camp PR Puerto Rican
D Division PS Philippine Scouts
Eng Engineer POE Port of Embarkation
FA Field Artillery RA Regular Army
GHQ General Headquarters RAI Regular Army Inactive
H Headquarters Regt Regiment
HD Horse drawn Rwy Railway
HHB Headquarters/Headquarter Battery TA Territory of Alaska
HHC Headquarters/Headquarter Company TH Territory of Hawaii
HHT Headquarters/Headquarter Troop TD Tractor/truck drawn
HT Heavy tractor
Inf Infantry TC Training Camp
MOB Mobilization Site QM Quartermaster
NCO Non Commissioned Officer

US Army Unit Organizational Symbols

Symbol	Name	Symbol	Name	Symbol	Name	Symbol	Name
⊠	Infantry	◻	Cavalry	⬤	Field Artillery	⬤	Coast Artillery Railway
E	Engineer	⊞	Medical	Q	Quartermaster	⋈	Air Service
X X X	Corp	X X	Division	X	Brigade	III	Regiment
II	Battalion/ Squadron	I	Company/ Troop/ Battery	•••	Platoon	••	Section

BIBLIOGRAPHY

Clay, Steven E., LTC (Ret), U.S. Army Order of Battle 1919-1941, Combat Studies Institute Press

Coffman, Edward M. The Regulars, The Belknap Press of Harvard University Press, 2004

Cornebise, Alfred Emile, The United States 15th Infantry Regiment in China, 1912-1938
McFarland & Company, Inc., Publishers, 2004

Linn, Brian McAllister, Guardians of Empire, The University of North Carolina Press, 1997

The Members of the 31st Infantry Regiment Association, The 31st Infantry Regiment,
McFarland & Company, Inc., Publishers, 2018

Truscott, Lucian K. Jr., The Twilight of the U.S. Cavalry, University Press of Kansas, 1989

Wilson, John B., Maneuver and Firepower, University Press of the Pacific, 2001

www.ingramcontent.com/pod-product-compliance
Lightning Source LLC
Chambersburg PA
CBHW071009120626
46546CB00003B/1000